© Danann Media Publishing Ltd 2024

First published in the UK by Sona Books, an imprint of Danann Media Publishing Limited

Published under licence from Future Publishing Limited a Future PLC group company.
All rights reserved. No part of this publication may be reproduced stored in a retrieval system or transmitted in any form or by any means without the prior written permission of the publisher.

Original material Copyright © 2023 by Future Publishing PLC.

Not to be reproduced without permission.

WARNING: For private domestic use only, any unauthorised copying, hiring, lending or public performance of this book is illegal.

CAT NO. SON0593

Proof reader: Cameron Thurlow

Photographs: All copyrights and trademarks are recognised and respected

Every effort has been made to acknowledge correctly and contact the source and/or copyright holder of each picture and Sona Books apologises for any unintentional errors or omissions, which will be corrected in future editions of the book.

All rights reserved. No part of this title may be reproduced or transmitted in any material form (including photocopying or storing it in any medium by electronic means and whether or not transiently or incidentally to some other use of this publication) without the written permission of the copyright owner, except in accordance with the provisions of the Copyright, Designs and Patents Act 1988. Applications for the copyright owner's written permission should be addressed to the publisher.

Made in EU.

ISBN: 978-1-915343-44-4

Welcome to
Quick & Easy
KNITTING

Knitting holds a warm place in many people's hearts as they fondly remember their grandmother knitting toys and clothing for them when they were children. But now, knitting is coming into its own.

In *Quick & Easy Knitting*, learn the basics and take on projects to liven up your home and wardrobe, or create heirlooms that you can pass down through the generations. After all, it only takes a pair of needles and some yarn...

Quick & Easy KNITTING

Contents

CHILDREN

10
Knitted cakes

12
Ballet-style wrap

16
Garter stitch hat & booties

18
Owl hat and mitts

20
Welcome baby card

24
Coat hangers

26
Dummy holders

CLOTHING

30
Simple tunic

32
Cosy cowl

33
Ribbed scarf

34
Weekender hat

36
Cotton top

39
Lace shawl

42
Chunky ribbed hat

44
Gradient shawl

16
Hat & wrist-warmers

50
Fingerless mitts

52
Garter stitch scarf

54
Staggered beanie

56
Knitted socks

58
Moss stitch neck warmer

60
Cosy mittens

62
Eyelit twigs top

66
Stormy waters shawl

70
Fairy tale legwarmers

72
Simple lace scarf

76
Picot-topped ankle socks

78
Fair Isle boot cuffs

Contents 7

HOME

82
Graduating stripes place mat

84
Trio of dishcloths

86
Placemat & coasters

87
I-cord coasters

88
Simple cushion

89
Gadget cosies

90
Textured draught excluder

92
Basket stitch container

94
Blackberry stitch tea cosy

96
Bobbles tea cosy

98
Chevron cushion cover

100
Willowherb lace doily

102
Simple baby blankets

104
Strawberry pie blanket

HOLIDAYS

110
Tilia Heart

112
Little carrot pouch

114
Easter egg decorations

116
Pumpkin place-holder

118
Snowflake cushion cover

120
Chunky cabled wreath

REFERENCE

124
Yarns

126
Knitting needles

128
Knitting kit bag

130
Yarn labels

131
Choosing yarn colours

132
Knitting abbreviations

133
Stitch symbol charts

134
Stitch patterns

139
Glossary

Children

Children

PATTERNS

10
Knitted cakes

12
Ballet-style wrap

16
Garter stitch hat & booties

18
Owl hat and mitts

20
Welcome baby card

24
Coat hangers

26
Dummy holders

Knitted cakes

Create these fun knitted cakes – all calorie free!

What you need

FOR THE SET

1 x 50g (125m) ball of Scheepjes Catona (100% cotton) in each of:
- White (Snow White 106)
- Pink (Powder Pink 238)
- Beige (Linen 505)
- Pair of 2.75mm (No. 12) knitting needles
- Washable toy stuffing
- Selection of buttons and beads for decoration

TENSION

30 stitches and 40 rows, to 10 x 10cm, over reverse stocking stitch, using 2.75mm needles.

ABBREVIATIONS

K, knit; **p**, purl; **st(s)**, stitch(es); **tog**, together; **inc**, increase (by working twice into same st); **pwise**, purlwise (as if to purl); **rss**, reverse stocking **st** (p on right side and **k** on wrong side)

Striped case cupcake

SIDES

With 2.75mm needles and White, cast on 12 sts.
With White, k 2 rows.
Change to Pink. K 2 rows.
Repeat last 4 rows, 23 times more.
With White, cast off, but do not break off yarn.

TOP RIM

With right side facing, using 2.75mm needles and attached yarn, pick up and k49 sts evenly along row-end edge. K 1 row.
Next row: K1, [place st on right needle back onto left needle and k2tog] to end. Fasten off.

BASE

With right side facing, using 2.75mm needles and White, pick up and k49 sts evenly along other row-end edge. P 1 row.
1st decrease row: K1, [k2tog, k4] 8 times – 41 sts.
P 1 row.
2nd decrease row: K1, [k2tog, k3] 8 times – 33 sts.
P 1 row.
3rd decrease row: K1, [k2tog, k2] 8 times – 25 sts.
P 1 row.
4th decrease row: K1, [k2tog, k1] 8 times – 17 sts.
P 1 row.
5th decrease row: K1, [k2tog] 8 times – 9 sts.
Break off yarn, thread end through remaining sts, pull up tightly and secure.

Cake

With right side facing, using 2.75mm needles and Beige, and holding rim folded forward towards you, pick up and k49 sts evenly along row-end edge of side.
Increase row: P3, inc pwise in next st, [p5, inc pwise in next st] 7 times, p3 – 57 sts.
K 1 row and p 1 row.

Icing

Join in White.
1st decrease row: K1, [k2tog, k5] 8 times – 49 sts.
Beginning with a k row, rss 4 rows.
2nd decrease row: K1, [k2tog, k4] 8 times – 41 sts.
Rss 3 rows.
3rd decrease row: K1, [k2tog, k3] 8 times – 33 sts.
P 1 row.
4th decrease row: K1, [k2tog, k2] 8 times – 25 sts.
5th decrease row: P1, [p2tog, p1] 8 times – 17 sts.
6th decrease row: K1, [k2tog] 8 times – 9 sts.
Break off yarn, thread end through remaining sts, pull up tightly and secure.

NOTE

If making as a toy, use yarn to embroider French knots, instead of using buttons and beads. Finished size may vary slightly, depending on amount of toy stuffing used. Yarn amounts are based on average requirements and are therefore approximate. Figures in square brackets are worked as stated after 2nd bracket.

Children | 11

To make up

Join seam, leaving an opening. Stuff firmly and close opening. Sew on buttons and beads as desired on top of icing, using the photo as a guide.

Pink case cupcake
Using Pink throughout for sides, top rim and base, work as striped case cupcake.

White case cupcake
Using White throughout for sides, top rim and base and Pink for icing, work as striped case cupcake.

Quick & Easy KNITTING

Ballet-style wrap

We love this top knitted in pink or white.
What would your colour choice be?

What you need

FOR THE WRAP
3 (3) (4) (4) (4) (5) (5) (5) x 25g
(200m) ball of Wendy Air (70% kid
mohair, 30% nylon) in each of:
- Pink (Joy 2617)
- White (Celeste 2610)
- Pair of 3mm (No. 11)
  knitting needles
- Pair of 3.75mm (No. 9)
  knitting needles
- 1 stitch holder

TENSION
22 stitches and 32 rows, to 10 x 10cm,
over pattern, using 3.75mm needles.

ABBREVIATIONS
St(s), stitch(es); **k**, knit; **p**, purl; **nil**,
meaning nothing can be worked
here for this size; **tog**, together
(decrease, by working as many sts
together as stated); **dec**, decrease 1
st (by working k2tog on a k row and
p2tog on a p row); **inc**, increase 1 st
(by working into same st twice)

Ballet-style wrap

BACK

With 3mm needles, cast on 71 (73) (75)
(77) (83) (89) (95) (101) sts.
1st rib row: K1, [p1, k1] to end.
2nd rib row: P1, [k1, p1] to end.
Last 2 rows form rib. Rib a further 4 (4)
(4) (8) (8) (8) (8) (8) rows.
Change to 3.75mm needles.
1st pattern row: K1 (2) (1) (2) (1) (2) (1)
(2), [p1, k3] to last 2 (3) (2) (3) (2) (3)
(2) (3) sts, p1, k1 (2) (1) (2) (1) (2) (1) (2).
2nd pattern row: P.
3rd pattern row: P nil (1) (nil) (1) (nil) (1)
(nil) (1), [k3, p1] to last 3 (nil) (3) (nil) (3)
(nil) (3) (nil) sts, k3 (nil) (3) (nil) (3) (nil)
(3) (nil).
4th pattern row: P.
Last 4 rows form pattern. Continue in
pattern as follows,
Inc 1 st at each end of next and
3 (5) (7) (9) (9) (9) (9) (9) following 3rd
rows – 79 (85) (91) (97) (103) (109) (115)
(121) sts.
Pattern a further 32 (30) (24) (20) (20)
(20) (20) (20)
rows straight.

Shape armholes: Keeping pattern
correct, cast off 4 (5) (5) (6) (6) (7) (7)
(8) sts at beginning of next 2 rows – 71
(75) (81) (85) (91) (95) (101) (105) sts.
Dec 1 st at each end of next 3 (3) (3) (3)
(5) (5) (5) (5) rows, then at each end of
following 2 (2) (3) (3) (2) (2) (3) (4)
alternate rows – 61 (65) (69) (73) (77)
(81) (85) (87) sts.
Pattern a further 37 (41) (39) (41) (41)
(43) (41) (41) rows straight.
Shape shoulders: Cast off 9 (9) (10)
(10) (11) (11) (12) (12) sts at beginning of
next 2 rows, then 9 (10) (10) (11) (11) (12)
(12) (13) sts at beginning of following 2
rows
– 25 (27) (29) (31) (33) (35) (37) (37)
sts.
Slip remaining sts onto a st holder.

LEFT FRONT

With 3mm needles, cast on 71 (73) (75)
(77) (83) (89) (95) (101) sts.
Rib 6 (6) (6) (10) (10) (10) (10) (10) rows
as given for back.
Change to 3.75mm needles.
Work 1st pattern row as given
for back. **

Size		66 / 26	71 / 28	76 / 30	81 / 32	86 / 36	91 / 36	97 / 38	102 / 40
Size	cm / in	66 / 26	71 / 28	76 / 30	81 / 32	86 / 36	91 / 36	97 / 38	102 / 40
Actual measurements	cm / in	72 / 28¼	77 / 30¼	82½ / 32½	88 / 34½	93½ / 36¾	99 / 39	104½ / 41¼	110 / 43¼

NOTE

If preferred, to accommodate the large amount of sts for the front border, you can use a long circular needle instead of straight
needles. Yarn amounts are based on average requirements and are therefore approximate. Instructions are given for small size.
Where they vary, work figures in round brackets for larger sizes. Instructions in square brackets are worked as stated after 2nd bracket.

Children | 13

Continue in pattern as given for back and shape front neck as follows,

Shape front neck: **2nd row:** P1, p2tog, p to end – 70 (72) (74) (76) (82) (88) (94) (100) sts.

3rd row: K3 (nil) (3) (nil) (3) (nil) (3) (nil), [p1, k3] to last 3 (4) (3) (4) (3) (4) (3) (4) sts, p nil (1) (nil) (1) (nil) (1) (nil) (1), k2tog, k1 – 69 (71) (73) (75) (81) (87) (93) (99) sts.

4th row: P.

Keeping pattern correct, shape side and continue to shape front neck as follows,

1st row: Inc in next st, pattern to last 3 sts, k2tog, k1.

2nd row: P1, p2tog, p to end – 1 st decreased.

3rd row: Pattern to end.

4th row: P1 p2tog, p to last st, inc in last st.

5th row: Pattern to last 3 sts, k2tog, k1 – 1 st decreased.

6th row: P.

Repeat the last 6 rows, 1 (2) (3) (4) (4) (4) (4) (4) time(s) more – 65 (65) (65) (65) (71) (77) (83) (89) sts.

Keeping pattern correct, dec at neck edge on next 2 rows, then pattern 1 row straight.

Repeat the last 3 rows, until you have 45 (47) (51) (53) (59) (65) (71) (77) sts.

2nd & 3rd sizes only: Work 1 further row, decreasing at neck edge – (46) (50) sts.

All sizes: *** Continue to decrease at neck edge on 2 of every 3 rows as before and at the same time, shape armhole as follows,

Shape armhole: Cast off 4 (5) (5) (6) (6) (7) (7) (8) sts at beginning of next row.

Work 1 row.

Dec 1 st at armhole edge on next 3 (3) (3) (3) (5) (5) (5) (5) rows and then on following 2 (2) (3) (3) (2) (2) (3) (4) alternate rows.

Continue to decrease on neck edge on 2 of every 3 rows as before until you have 18 (19) (20) (21) (22) (23) (24) (25) sts.

Pattern straight until front matches back before shoulder shaping, ending at armhole edge.

Shape shoulders: Cast off 9 (9) (10) (10) (11) (11) (12) (12) sts at beginning of next row – 9 (10) (10) (11) (11) (12) (12) (13) sts.

Pattern 1 row. Cast off.

RIGHT FRONT

Work as given for left front to **.

Continue in pattern as given for back and shape front neck as follows,

2nd row: P to last 3 sts, p2tog, p1 – 70 (72) (74) (76) (82) (88) (94) (100) sts.

3rd row: K1 k2tog, pattern to end – 69 (71) (73) (75) (81) (87) (93) (99) sts.

4th row: P.

Keeping pattern correct, shape side and continue to shape front neck as follows,

1st row: K1, k2tog, pattern to last st, inc in last st.

2nd row: P to last 3 sts, p2tog, p1.

3rd row: Pattern to end.

4th row: Inc in next st, p to last 3 sts, p2tog, p1.

5th row: K1, k2tog, pattern to end.

6th row: P.

Repeat the last 6 rows, 1 (2) (3) (4) (4) (4) (4) (4) time(s) more – 65 (65) (65) (65) (71) (77) (83) (89) sts.

Keeping pattern correct, dec at neck edge on next 2 rows, then pattern 1 row straight.

Repeat the last 3 rows, until you have 45 (47) (51) (53) (59) (65) (71) (77) sts.

Dec on neck edge of next 1 (2) (2) (1) (1) (1) (1) (1) row(s) – 44 (45) (49) (52) (58) (64) (70) (76) sts.

Work as given for left front from *** to end.

SLEEVES (BOTH ALIKE)

With 3mm needles, cast on 27 (31) (35) (39) (43) (43) (47) (49) sts.

Rib 5 (5) (5) (9) (9) (9) (9) (9) rows as given for back.

Next row: Increase row: Rib 2 (4) (6) (3) (5) (5) (7) (5), inc in next st, [rib 1 (1) (1) (2) (2) (2) (2) (2), inc in next st] to last 2 (4) (6) (2) (4) (4) (6) (4) sts, rib to end – 39 (43) (47) (51) (55) (55) (59) (63) sts.

Change to 3.75mm needles.

1st pattern row: K1, [p1, k3] to last 2 sts, p1, k1.

2nd pattern row: P.

3rd pattern row: [K3, p1] to last 3 sts, k3.

4th pattern row: P.

Last 4 rows form pattern. Continue in pattern, and work increase sts into pattern as follows, Inc 1 st at each end of next row and 13 (13) (11) (12) (10) (12) (10) (10) following 6th (6th) (8th) (8th) (10th) (8th) (10th) (10th) rows – 67 (71) (71) (77) (77) (81) (81) (85) sts.

Pattern a further 13 (21) (11) (15) (11) (15) (11) (11) rows straight.

Shape sleeve top: Cast off 4 (5) (5) (6) (6) (7) (7) (8) sts at beginning of next 2 rows – 59 (61) (61) (65) (65) (67) (67) (69) sts.

Dec 1 st at each end of next 3 (3) (3) (3) (5) (5) (5) (5) rows, then on 4 (5) (5) (8) (8) (10) (10) (11) following alternate rows and then on each of next 15 (15) (15) (13) (11) (9) (9) (9) rows – 15 (15) (15) (17) (17) (19) (19) (19) sts.

TIES (BOTH ALIKE)

With 3mm needles, cast on 7 (7) (7) (11) (11) (11) (11) (11) sts.

1st rib row: K1, [p1, k1] to end.

2nd rib row: K2, [p1, k1] to last st, k1.

Last 2 rows form rib. Rib a further 116 (126) (136) (148) (162) (174) (186) (198) rows.

Cast off in rib.

FRONT BORDER

Join shoulder seams.
With right side facing and with 3mm needles, pick up and k112 (119) (119) (131) (131) (141) (141) (147) sts evenly from top of rib up right front to shoulder seam, k across 25 (27) (29) (31) (33) (35) (37) (37) sts from back st holder, pick up and k112 (119) (119) (131) (131) (141) (141) (147) sts evenly from shoulder seam down left front to top of rib – 249 (265) (267) (293) (295) (317) (319) (331) sts.
Rib 5 (5) (5) (7) (7) (7) (7) (7) rows as given for back.
Cast off in rib.

To make up

Set in sleeves and join sleeve seams. Leaving an opening in the rib at right side of approximately 1.5 (1.5) (1.5) (2) (2) (2) (2) (2) cm for tie, join side seams. Sew cast-on edge of ties to row-ends of rib on fronts. Cross right front over left and slot tie at left front through opening in rib to tie both ties together at back.

Garter stitch hat & booties

The hat is perfect for beginners in simple garter stitch. Then try your hand at the booties

Children

What you need

FOR THE SET
1 (1) (1) (1) x 100g (310m) ball of King Cole Comfort DK (60% Acrylic, 40% Nylon) in:
- Silver (772)
- Oddments of White DK yarn for embroidery

FOR THE HAT
- Pair of 4mm (No. 8) knitting needles.

FOR THE BOOTIES
- Pair of 3.25mm (No. 10) knitting needles for first size and pair of 4mm (No. 8) knitting needles for second size

TENSION
22 stitches and 40 rows, to 10 x 10cm, over garter stitch, using 4mm needles.

ABBREVIATIONS
St(s), stitch(es); **k**, knit; **p**, purl; **gst**, garter stitch (every row k); **inc**, increase 1 st (by working into back and front of the same st); **dec**, decrease 1 st, by working k2tog on a k row and p2tog on a p row; **ss**, stocking st (k on right side and p on wrong side); **tog**, together

NOTE ----------------------
Hat seam is placed at centre back and 4cm brim is folded up before embroidery. Yarn amounts are based on average requirements and are therefore approximate. Instructions are given for small size. Where they vary, work figures in round brackets for larger sizes.

Size Hat	months	0-6	6-12	12-18	24-36
Width around head	cm in	34 13½	37 14½	39.5 15½	42 16½
Size Booties	months	0-6	6-12		
Actual measurements Foot length	cm in	9 3½	10 4		

Yarn: 100g (310m) ball of King Cole Comfort DK (60% Acrylic, 40% Nylon)				
Yarn A Silver (772)	1	1	1	1

Hat
Worked in one piece, with a folded brim.
With Silver and 4mm needles, cast on 75 (79) (84) (90) sts. Gst until hat measures 19.5 (20.5) (21.5) (21.5) cm, ending with a right side row. Cast off.

To make up
Join back seam, reversing seam for a 4cm turn-back brim. With back seam in centre, sew top seam. With White held double, embroider hat with cross stitch.

Booties (make 2)

SOLE
Starting at side of foot.
With Silver and 3.25mm needles for first size and 4mm needles for second size, cast on 14 sts. Gst 8 rows, inc 1 st at each end of 2nd and every following alternate row – 22 sts. Gst another 5 rows.
Gst 7 rows, dec 1 st at each end of next and every following alternate row – 14 sts.

UPPER
Next row: Cast on 5 sts (for heel), k to end – 19 sts.
Gst 7 rows, inc 1 st at beginning of next and every following alternate row – 23 sts.

Next row: Cast off 12 sts, k to end – 11 sts.
Gst 11 rows.
Next row: Cast on 12 sts, k to end – 23 sts.
Gst 7 rows, dec 1 st at beginning of next and every following alternate row – 19 sts. Cast off.

LEG
With Silver and 3.25mm needles for first size and 4mm needles for second size, beginning at the second cast-on edge of heel, pick up and k12 sts evenly along edge to centre front of bootee, pick up and k6 sts across centre, and finally, pick up and k12 sts evenly along first cast-off edge of heel – 30 sts. Gst 19 rows.

INNER
Beginning with a k row, ss 10 rows. Cast off.

To make up
Fold stocking stitch inner to inside, and sew in place at base of gst cuff. Join heel seam. Pin upper to sole, easing excess upper around toe and sew in position. With White held double, embroider cuff with cross stitch.

Owl hat and mitts

Learn how to make these hootingly adorable items
that are perfect birthday or baby shower gifts

What you need

FOR THE SET

1 (1) (1) (1) (1) x 50g (160m) Peter
Pan DK 50g (160m) ball(s) in:

- Blue Jeans
- Jade
- White
- Pair of 2-3¼mm (No. 3) knitting
  needles

TENSION

24 sts and 32 rows = 10cm (4in) in
stocking stitch on 4mm needles.

ABBREVIATIONS

K, knit; **p**, purl; **st(s)**, stitch(es); **tog**,
together; **inc**, increase (by working
twice into same st); **pwise**, purlwise
(as if to purl); **rss**, reverse stocking
st (p on right side and **k** on wrong
side)

Hat

Using 3¼mm needles and col 2, cast
(bind) on 73 (79, 85, 91, 97) sts.
Row 1: K1, * P1, K1, rept from * to end.
Row 2: P1, * K1, P1, rept from * to end.
These two rows form rib, repeat 1st and
2nd row three times more.
Change to 4mm needles and join in A.
Now, working in st st throughout, and
commencing with a K row, work 2 rows
in col 1 then 2 rows in col 2.
Last 4 rows set stripe pattern, repeat
these 4 rows 3 (3, 4, 5, 5) times more.
Break off col 2, and continue in col 1
only.

Size Hat		S	M	L	XL	XXL
Width around head	cm	33	35.5	38	41	43
	in	13	14	15	16	17
Size Booties	months	prem	0	6	12	24

Yarn: Peter Pan DK 50g (160m) ball(s)					
Yarn A Blue Jeans	1	1	1	1	1
Yarn B Jade	1	1	1	1	1
Yarn B White	1	1	1	1	1

Continue in st st until hat measures 12
(12, 13, 14, 14)cm, 4¾ (4¾, 5¼, 5½, 5½)ins
from cast (bind)-on edge ending on a
P row.
Cast (bind) off.

EYES (MAKE 2)

Using 4mm needles and col 3, cast
(bind) on 3 sts.
Row 1: [Inc in next st], rept in each st to
end. 6 sts.
Row 2: [Inc in next st], rept in each st to
end. 12 sts.
Row 3: K1, * inc in next st , K1 rept from *
to last st, K1. 17 sts.
Row 4: K1, * inc in next st , K1 rept from *
to end. 25 sts.
Cast (bind) off.
Join row end edges, work will then
form a circle.

INNER EYES (MAKE 2)

Using 4mm needles and col 2, cast
(bind) on 5 sts.
Row 1: Sl 1, P3, sl 1.
Row 2: K5
Row 3: Sl 1, P3, sl 1

Row 4: K5
Cast (bind) off pwise.
Run a gathering stitch around outer
edge, and gather up to form a small
berry shape.

BEAK

Using 4mm needles and col 2, cast
(bind) on 2 sts.
Row 1: Purl.
Row 2: K1, m1, K1.
Row 3: P3.
Row 4: K1, m1, K1, m1, K1.
Row 5: P5.
Cast (bind) off.

To make up

Using the photograph as a
guide, and placing the beak at
centre of work, attach eyes and
beak as shown.
 Fold in side edges of hat so
that they meet at centre back.
Join back seam and top seam
by top sewing.

Children 19

Pattern by
Thomas B Ramsden
This pattern was kindly supplied by Thomas B Ramsden, a family business who are the suppliers of Wendys and Peter Pan, two of the biggest brands of yarn in the UK.
www.tbramsden.co.uk

Mitts
Using 4mm needles and col 1, cast (bind) on 26(26, 28, 28, 30) sts.
Row 1: * K1, P1, rept from * to end
Repeat this row 5 times more.
Row 7: (Make eyelet holes) K1, * yo, K2tog, rept from * to last st, K1.
Next row: Purl to end.
Continue in st st for a further 20 (22, 24, 28, 30) rows, ending with a purl row.
Cast (bind) off loosely.

EYES (MAKE 2)
Using 4mm needles and col 3, cast (bind) on 3 sts.
Row 1: [Inc in next st], rept in each st to end. 6 sts.
Row 2: [Inc in next st], rept in each st to end. 12sts.
Row 3: K1, * inc in next st, K1 rept from * to last st, K1. (18sts)
Cast (bind) off.
Join row end edges, work will then form a circle.

INNER EYES (MAKE 2)
Work as given for inner eyes of hat.

BEAK
Work as given for beak of hat.

To make up
Fold mitten in half, so the seam is at one side.
Using the photograph as a guide, attach eyes and beak as shown.
Join side and top seam by top sewing.
Using col 2 and col 3, make a twisted cord and thread through eyelet holes.

Welcome baby card

The perfect handmade way to welcome the new baby in your life

What you need

FOR THE SET

Small amount of 4 ply in each of:
- Pink
- Green
- Lilac
- Yellow
- Length of narrow white ribbon
- 2 small buttons
- Pair of 2mm (No. 14) knitting needles
- Size A3 medium-weight card folded in half and decorated as desired
- Pair of 23cm-long wooded dowels
- 40cm length of DK cotton for washing line
- 13 mini wooden pegs
- Sticky pads

TENSION

36 stitches and 48 rows, to 10 x 10cm over stocking stitch, using 2mm needles.

ABBREVIATIONS

K, knit; **p**, purl; **st**, stitch; **tog**, together; **sl**, slip; **psso**, pass sl st over; **ss**, stocking stitch (k on right side and p on wrong side); **gst**, garter st (every row k); **mst**, moss st; **yf**, yarn forward to make a st; **yrn**, yarn round needle to make a st

Shawl

Centre: With 2mm needles and White, cast on 23 sts.
1st row: K4, [yf, sl1, k2tog, psso, yf, k3] twice, yf, sl1, k2tog, psso, yf, k4.
2nd row: P.
3rd row: K1, [yf, sl1, k2tog, psso, yf, k3] 3 times, yf, sl1, k2tog, psso, yf, k1.
4th row: P.
Pattern another 42 rows. Cast off.
Edging: With 2mm needles and White, cast on 4 sts. K 1 row.
1st row: K2, yf, k2 – 5 sts.
2nd row: K.
3rd row: K3, yf, k2 – 6 sts.
4th row: Cast off 2, k to end – 4 sts.
These 4 rows form pattern. Continue in pattern until straight edge of edging fits around outer edges of centre, allowing extra for each corner, ending with 3rd row. Cast off. Sew edging to centre, then join first 4 sts on cast-on and cast-off edges together.

Dress

SKIRT

With 2mm needles and Pink, cast on 35 sts. P 3 rows.
1st row: K1, [yf, sl1, k2tog, psso, yf, k3] to last 4 sts, yf, sl1, k2tog, psso, yf, k1.
2nd row: P.
3rd row: K4, [yf, sl1, k2tog, psso, yf, k3] to last 7 sts, yf, sl1, k2tog, psso, yf, k4.
4th row: P.
Repeat these 4 rows, twice more.
Dec row: K1, k2tog, k1, [k2tog, k2] to

Children 21

last 3 sts, k2tog, k1 – 26 sts.
Eyelet row: P2, [yrn, p2tog] to end.
P 1 row.

BODICE

Dividing row: P7, turn and work on these sts only for right back.

RIGHT BACK

Beginning with a k row,
ss 8 rows. Cast off.
Return to end of dividing row, join in yarn and p13 sts, turn and work on these sts for front.

FRONT

Beginning with a k row, ss 3 rows.
Shape neck: Next row: P5, cast off 3, p to end. Work on last set of 5 sts only for left side. K 1 row.
Cast off 2 sts at beginning of next row – 3 sts. Ss 2 rows. Cast off.
With right side facing, rejoin yarn at inside edge to remaining 5 sts of front for right side. Ss 2 rows.
Cast off 2 sts at beginning of next row.
P 1 row. Cast off.
Rejoin yarn at inside edge to remaining 6 sts for left back and p to end.

LEFT BACK

Beginning with a k row,
ss 8 rows. Cast off.
Sleeves (both alike): With 2mm needles and Pink, cast on 10 sts. P 2 rows.
Inc row: P1, inc pwise in each of next 4 sts, p1, inc pwise in each of next 3 sts, p1 – 17 sts.
1st row: K1, [yf, sl1, k2tog, psso, yf, k3] twice, yf, sl1, k2tog, psso, yf, k1.
2nd row: P.
3rd row: K4, yf, sl1, k2tog, psso, yf, k3, yf, sl1, k2tog, psso, yf, k4.
4th row: P. Cast off.
Join shoulder and sleeve seams. Sew in sleeves. Join back seam on skirt and bodice. Thread length of ribbon through eyelet holes, bringing ends at centre front and tie into a bow.

T-shirt

BACK

With 2mm needles and Green, cast on 13 sts.
1st rib row: K1, [p1, k1] to end.
2nd rib row: P1, [k1, p1] to end.
Beginning with a k row, ss 8 rows.
Shape sleeves: 1st row: Cast on 6 sts, k to end.
2nd row: Cast on 6 sts, k2, p to last 2 sts, k2 – 25 sts.
Keeping the 2 sts at each end in gst and remainder in ss, work 3 rows.
Shape neck: Next row: K2, p7, cast off next 7 sts, p to last 2 sts, k2.
Work on last set of 9 sts only for right front neck.
Right front neck: Work 2 rows.
Next row: K7, inc in next st, k1.
Next row: Inc in first st, p7, k2.
Next row: K9, inc in next st, k1 – 12 sts.
Break off yarn.

LEFT FRONT NECK

Rejoin yarn at inside edge to remaining 9 sts and ss 2 rows.
Next row: Inc in first st, k8.
Next row: K2, p6, inc in next st, p1.
Next row: Inc in first st, k10 – 12 sts.
Joining row: K2, p9, inc in next st across sts of left front neck, then p10, k2, across sts of right front neck – 25 sts.
Work 2 rows.
Cast off 6 sts at beginning of next 2 rows – 13 sts.
Ss another 8 rows.
Rib 2 rows as before. Cast off in rib.
Fold T-shirt in half and join side and underarm seams.

Bonnet

With 2mm needles and Pink, cast on 17 sts.
K 1 row.
1st row: K1, [yf, sl1, k2tog, psso, yf, k3] twice, yf, sl1, k2tog, psso, yf, k1.
2nd row: P.
3rd row: K4, yf, sl1, k2tog, psso, yf, k3, yf, sl1, k2tog, psso, yf, k4.

4th row: P.

1st dec row: K1, [k2tog, k2] 4 times – 13 sts. K 1 row.

2nd dec row: K1, [k2tog, k1] 4 times – 9 sts. K 1 row.

3rd dec row: K1, [k2tog] 4 times – 5 sts. Break off yarn and thread end through remaining sts, pull up tightly and secure. Join back seam from gathered end to

3rd row of lace pattern. Cut two 4cm lengths of ribbon. Sew one to each corner on bonnet. Tie ends into a bow.

Booties (make 2)
CUFF

With 2mm needles and White, cast on 2 sts. K 1 row.

1st row: K1, yf, k1 – 3 sts.

2nd row: K.

3rd row: K2, yf, k1 – 4 sts.

4th row: Cast off 2, k to end – 2 sts. Repeat these 4 rows, 3 times more, then work 1st to 3rd rows again. Cast off.

MAIN PIECE

With 2mm needles and White, pick up and k12 sts along straight edge of edging.

SHAPE INSTEP

Next 2 rows: K8, turn, p4, turn. Ss 4 rows on these 4 sts only.

Break off yarn and rejoin yarn at base of instep, pick up and k3 sts from first side of instep, k4 sts from top of instep, pick up and k3 sts from other side of instep, then k remaining 4 sts – 18 sts. K 1 row.

1st dec row: K2, [skpo, k2] twice, [k2tog, k2] twice – 14 sts. K 1 row.

2nd dec row: K5, skpo, k2tog, k5 – 12 sts.
Cast off.

Fold bootie in half and join cast-off edge together for sole, then join back seam. Thread length of ribbon through sts at base of cuff, bringing ends at

centre top of instep and tie into a bow.

Trousers

With 2mm needles and Lilac, cast on 25 sts for waistband.

1st rib row: K1, [p1, k1] to end.

2nd rib row: P1, [k1, p1] to end. Beginning with a k row, ss 6 rows.

SHAPE CROTCH

1st row: Inc in first st, k11, inc in next st, k10, inc in next st, k1 – 28 sts.

2nd row: P13, inc in next st, p14 – 29 sts.

1st dec row: K2tog, k12, k2tog, k11, k2tog – 26 sts.

2nd dec row: P12, p2tog, p12 – 25 sts.

Dividing row: K12, cast off 1, k to end. Work on last 12 sts only for first leg.

FIRST LEG

Ss 9 rows. Work 2 rows in k1, p1 rib. Cast off in rib.

SECOND LEG

With wrong side facing, rejoin yarn to remaining 12 sts.

Ss 9 rows.

Work 2 rows in k1, p1 rib.

Cast off in rib.

Join leg seams to crotch, then join back seam.

Jacket
BACK AND FRONTS

With 2mm needles and Yellow, cast on 33 sts.

Mst row: K1, [p1, k1] to end. Mst another 9 rows.

Dividing row: Mst 8, turn and work on these sts only for right front.

Right front: Mst another 11 rows.

Next row: Mst 3, cast off last 5 sts for shoulder. Break off yarn.

BACK

Return to end of dividing row, rejoin yarn at inside edge to remaining sts,

mst 17 sts, turn. Mst another 11 rows.

Next row: Cast off 5 sts, mst to last 5 sts, cast off last 5 sts. Break off yarn.

LEFT FRONT

Rejoin yarn at inside edge to remaining 8 sts and mst to end. Mst another 11 rows.

Next row: Cast off 5 sts, mst to end.

COLLAR

Mst 3 sts from left front, 7 sts from back and 3 sts from right front – 13 sts. Mst 2 rows. Cast off in mst.

SLEEVES (BOTH ALIKE)

With 2mm needles and Yellow, cast on 17 sts.

Mst row: K1, [p1, k1] to end. Mst 1 row. Inc and work into mst, 1 st at each end of next row and following alternate row – 21 sts. Mst another 5 rows. Cast off in mst. Join shoulder seams. Sew cast-on edge of sleeves to armholes. Join sleeve seams. Make two small button loops on right front. Sew on buttons.

To make up

Attach ends of DK cotton to top of wooden poles. Arrange knitted items along the line and secure in position with pegs. Place small pieces of sticky pads evenly spaced along one side of each pole; stick poles 1cm away from edge on inside of card.

Coat hangers

Hang baby's clothes in style with these unique hangers

What you need

FOR THE SET

1 x 100g (295m) ball of Stylecraft Special DK (100% acrylic) in each of:
- Turquoise (1068)
- White (1001)
- Lemon (1020)
- Blue (Aster 1003)*
- Oddments of Black for embroidery
- Pair of 3mm (No. 11)
- 4mm (No. 8) knitting needles
- 3 x 27cm-wide coat hangers
- washable toy stuffing,
- 20 x 25cm polyester wadding for covering hangers

TENSION

26 stitches and 36 rows, to 10 x 10cm, over stocking stitch, using 3mm needles and 22 stitches, and 28 rows, to 10 x 10cm, over stocking stitch, using 4mm needles.

ABBREVIATIONS

K, knit; **p**, purl; **st**, stitch; **tog**, together; **dec**, decrease (by working 2 sts tog); **inc**, increase (by working twice into same st); **ss**, stocking st (k on right side and p on wrong side); **yf**, yarn forward to make a st

NOTE - - - - - - - - - - - - - - - - - - -

Yarn amounts are based on average requirements and are therefore approximate. Instructions in square brackets are worked as stated after.

Duck

HANGER COVER

With 4mm needles and Turquoise, cast on 11 sts.
P 1 row.
Inc row: [Inc in next st kwise] to end – 22 sts. Beginning with a p row, ss 37 rows.
Eyelet row: K10, yf, k2tog, k10.
Ss another 37 rows.
Dec row: [K2tog] to end – 11 sts.
P 1 row. Cast off.
Fold cover in half, lengthwise and join end seams. Cut a 10 x 25cm strip from wadding, making a hole in the centre for hanger hook to go through. Place wadding over hanger, then pushing hook through eyelet hole of knitted fabric, place cover over wadding and join seam, enclosing wadding.

HEAD

With 3mm needles and White, cast on 16 sts. P 1 row.
Next row: [Inc in next st kwise] to end – 32 sts. P 1 row.
Next row: K4, inc in next st, [k1, inc in next st] 3 times, k10, inc in next st, [k1, inc in next st] 3 times, k4 – 40 sts. Ss 3 rows.
Next row: K5, inc in next st, [k2, inc in next st] 3 times, k10, inc in next st, [k2, inc in next st] 3 times, k5 – 48 sts. Ss 11 rows.
Next row: K5, k2tog, [k2, k2tog] 3 times, k10, k2tog, [k2, k2tog] 3 times, k5 – 40 sts. Ss 3 rows.
Next row: K4, k2tog, [k1, k2tog] 3 times, k10, k2tog, [k1, k2tog] 3 times, k4 – 32 sts. P 1 row.
Next row: [K2tog] to end – 16 sts.
P 1 row. Cast off.

Fold head in half lengthwise, having seam at centre back, then join centre back seam. Join cast-on edge, stuff, then join remaining seam for top of head. With Black, embroider small vertical stitches for eyes, as shown in photo.

BEAK

With 3mm needles and Turquoise, cast on 9 sts.
Beginning with a k row, ss 2 rows.
Next row: [K1, k2tog] to end – 6 sts.
P 1 row. Break off yarn leaving a long end. Thread end through remaining sts, pull up tightly and fasten off securely.
Join row-ends together, stuff and sew cast-on edge to centre of face, just below eyes. Attach head to centre of hanger.

Pig

HANGER COVER

Work as given for duck's cover, using Lemon instead of Turquoise.
Head: Work as given for duck's head, using Turquoise instead of White.

SNOUT

With 3mm needles and White, cast on 16 sts.
Next row: [K2tog] to end – 8 sts.
Break off yarn leaving a long end. Thread end through remaining sts, pull up tightly and fasten off securely. Catch ends together, flatten and sew to centre of face, just below eyes. With Black, embroider two evenly-spaced vertical stitches on centre of snout for nostrils.

Children 25

EARS (MAKE 2)
With 3mm needles and Lemon, cast on 2 sts. P 1 row.
Next row: Inc, k1 – 3 sts. P 1 row.
Next row: [Inc] twice, k1 – 5 sts. P 1 row.
Next row: Inc, k2, inc, k1 – 7 sts. P 1 row. K 1 row. Cast off.
With tip of ears pointing to front of face, sew ears to top of head. Attach head to centre of hanger.

Lamb

HEAD
Work as given for duck's head, using Blue instead of White, and embroidering a Y-shape with Black for nose, just below eyes.

HEAD TRIM
With 3mm needles and Lemon, cast on 4 sts. P 1 row.
Next row: [Inc in next st kwise] to end – 8 sts. Ss 7 rows.
Next row: [K2tog] to end – 4 sts. Cast off.
Sew trim lengthwise across top of head, adding a little stuffing.

EARS (MAKE 2)
With 3mm needles and Turquoise, cast on 4 sts. P 1 row.
Next row: [Inc in next st kwise, k1] to end – 6 sts. Ss 3 rows.
Next row: [K1, k2tog] to end – 4 sts. Repeat last 6 rows, once more. Cast off. Fold ears in half widthwise, join side seams then join cast-on/cast-off edges together. Fold ears in half again at base edge folded edge so that ends meet in the middle and sew to head at each side of trim.

Attachment loop: With 3mm needles and Blue, cast on 10 sts.
Beginning with a k row, ss 2 rows. Cast off. Sew ends to centre at back of head near top, so that head can be placed over hanger hook. Hook head over hanger.

Dummy holders

It's time to say goodbye to losing dummies

What you need

DOG DUMMY HOLDER

Small amount of DK yarn in each of:
- Ecru
- Beige
- Light Brown
- Pale Pink
- Length of DK yarn in Dark Brown for embroidery

CAT DUMMY HOLDER

Small amount of DK yarn in each of:
- Grey
- Light Pink
- Ecru
- Oatmeal
- Length of DK yarn in Dark Brown for embroidery

FINISHED MEASUREMENTS

approximately 8cm/3in tall.

ABBREVIATIONS

K, knit; **p**, purl; **st**, stitch; **tog**, together; **sl**, slip; **inc**, increase (by working twice into same st); **dec**, decrease; **ss**, stocking st (k on right side and p on wrong side); **psso**, pass slip st over; **skpo**, (sl1, k1, psso)

NOTE

Yarn amounts are based on average requirements and are therefore approximate. Instructions in square brackets are worked as stated after.

Dog

BODY

With 2.75mm needles and Ecru, cast on 10 sts for base. P 1 row.
1st inc row: [Inc kwise in next st] to end – 20 sts. P 1 row.
2nd inc row: [Inc in next st, k1] to end – 30 sts. P 1 row.
3rd inc row: [Inc in next st, k2] to end – 40 sts. Beginning with a p row, ss 15 rows.
1st dec row: [K3, k2tog] to end – 32 sts. Ss 5 rows.
2nd dec row: [K2, k2tog] to end – 24 sts.
Ss 3 rows.
3rd dec row: [K2tog] to end – 12 sts. Break off yarn, thread end through remaining sts, pull up tightly and secure. Gather cast on edge, pull up tightly and secure, then join row-ends, leaving an opening. Stuff body lightly and close opening. With seam at back, flatten body and using length of Ecru, work couple of stab stitches through all layers 3cm up from lower end and 4 stitches in from side edges to denote arms.

MUZZLE

With 2.75mm needles and Beige, cast on 16 sts. P 1 row.
Dec row: [K2, k2tog] to end – 12 sts. Break off yarn, thread end through remaining sts, pull up tightly and secure, then join row-ends. Position muzzle on upper part of body and sew in place, stuffing it as you sew. With Dark Brown, work French knot for each eye just above muzzle, then work short back stitch on top of muzzle for nose tip.

EARS (MAKE 2)

With 2.75mm needles and Light Brown, cast on 10 sts.
Beginning with a p row, ss 5 rows.
Dec row: [K2tog] to end – 5 sts. Break off yarn, thread end through remaining sts, pull up tightly and secure, then join row-ends. Sew cast-on edge of ears at sides on top of body.

FEET (MAKE 2)

With 2.75mm needles and Light Brown, cast on 10 sts.
Break off yarn and thread end through sts on needle, pull up tightly and secure. Join short ends and sew to lower edge of body. With Light Brown, work three French knots evenly spaced above top of each foot for paws.

BAND

With 2.75mm needles and Pale Pink, cast on 8 sts. K 150 rows.
Next row: Skpo, k4, k2tog – 6 sts. K 1 row.
Next row: Skpo, k2, k2tog – 4 sts. K 4 rows. Cast off.

Cat

BODY AND MUZZLE

Using Grey instead of Ecru and Pale Pink instead of Beige, work as given for dog.

Pull one strand from length of Brown and use this strand to work 3 straight stitches at each side of nose on muzzle for whiskers.

OUTER EARS (MAKE 2)

With 2.75mm needles and Grey,

cast on 6 sts. P 1 row.
Next row: Skpo, k2, k2tog – 4 sts.
P 1 row.
Next row: Skpo, k2tog – 2 sts.
P2tog and fasten off.

INNER EARS (MAKE 2)

With 2.75mm needles and Ecru, cast on 5 sts. P 1 row.
Next row: Skpo, k1, k2tog – 3 sts.
P 1 row.
Next row: Sl1, k2tog, psso.
Fasten off.
Join inner ear to outer ear. Sew cast-on edge of ears at sides on top of body.

FEET (MAKE 2)

Using Pale Pink instead of Light Brown, work as given for dog.

BAND

Using Oatmeal instead of Pale Pink, work as band on dog dummy holder.

To make up

Insert narrow strap at shaped end of band through clip end and sew to back of band. Fold back other end for about 3.5cm and sew Velcro pieces in position. Place toy on.

Clothing
PATTERNS

30 Simple tunic

32 Cosy cowl

33 Ribbed scarf

34 Weekender hat

36 Cotton top

39 Lace shawl

42 Chunky ribbed hat

44 Gradient shawl

48 Hat & wrist-warmers

50 Fingerless mitts

52 Garter stitch scarf

54 Staggered beanie

56 Knitted socks

58 Moss stitch neck warmer

60 Cosy mittens

62 Eyelit twigs top

66 Stormy waters shawl

70 Fairy tale legwarmers

72 Simple lace scarf

76 Picot-topped ankle socks

78 Fair Isle boot cuffs

Simple tunic

Relax as you knit this simple tunic with calming, repetitive stitches

What you need

9 (10) (12) (13) (15) x 50g (140m) balls of King Cole Luxury Merino DK (100% merino wool) in:
- Teal (2634)
- Pair of 4mm (No. 8) knitting needles
- One circular 4mm (No. 8) knitting needle (to use on back for working in rows with large number of sts)
- Stitch holders

TENSION
28 stitches and 30 rows, to 10 x 10cm, over pattern, using 4mm needles.

ABBREVIATIONS
K, knit; **p**, purl; **st(s)**, stitch(es)

Size		S	M	L	XL	XXL
To fit bust	cm	82–86	92–97	102–107	112–117	122–127
	in	32–34	36–38	40–42	44–46	48–50
Actual bust	cm	100	110	120	130	140
	in	39½	43¼	47¼	51¼	55
Length to shoulder	cm	80	82	84	86	88
	in	31½	32¼	33	33¾	34¾

Yarn: 50g (140m) balls of King Cole Luxury Merino DK (100% merino wool)					
Teal (2634)	9	10	12	13	15

NOTE
Yarn amounts are based on average requirements and are therefore approximate. Instructions are given for small size. Where they vary, work figures in round brackets for larger sizes. Instructions in square brackets are worked as stated after 2nd bracket.

BACK
With 4mm circular needle, cast on 141 (155) (169) (183) (197) sts. Work backwards and forwards in rows:
1st rib row: K1, [p1, k1] to end.
2nd rib row: P1, [k1, p1] to end.
These 2 rows form rib.
Rib a further 6 rows.
Continue in pattern thus:
1st row: P1, [k1, p1] to end.
2nd row: K1, [p1, k1] to end.
3rd and 4th rows: As 1st and 2nd rows.
5th row: K1, [p1, k1] to end.
6th row: P1, [k1, p1] to end.
7th and 8th rows: As 5th and 6th rows.
Last 8 rows form pattern and are repeated throughout.
Pattern straight until back measures 76 (78) (80) (82) (84) cm from cast-on edge, ending with a wrong side row.
Shape upper arms and shoulders: Cast off 8 (9) (10) (11) (12) sts at beginning of next 12 rows – 45 (47) (49) (51) (53) sts.
Cast off remaining sts.

POCKET LININGS (MAKE 2)
With 4mm needles, cast on 39 sts. Pattern 56 rows as given for back, ending with an 8th row.
Leave sts on a st holder.

LEFT FRONT
** With 4mm needles, cast on 63 (69) (75) (81) (87) sts.
1st rib row: P1, [k1, p1] to end.
2nd rib row: K1, [p1, k1] to end.
These 2 rows form rib.
Rib a further 6 rows.
Continue in pattern thus:
1st row: K1, [p1, k1] to end.
2nd row: P1, [k1, p1] to end.
3rd and 4th rows: As 1st and 2nd rows.
5th row: P1, [k1, p1] to end.
6th row: K1, [p1, k1] to end.
7th and 8th rows: As 5th and 6th rows.
Last 8 rows form pattern and are repeated throughout.
Pattern straight until front measures 25cm from cast-on edge, ending with a 3rd pattern row. **
Place pocket lining: Next row: Pattern 16 (18) (20) (22) (24), cast off 39 sts, pattern to end.

Next row: Pattern 8 (12) (16) (20) (24), pattern across 39 sts of pocket lining, pattern 16 (18) (20) (22) (24).

Pattern straight until front measures 76 (78) (80) (82) (84) cm from cast-on edge, ending with a wrong side row.

Shape upper arms and shoulders:
Cast off 8 (9) (10) (11) (12) sts at beginning of next and 5 following right side rows – 15 sts.

Continue in pattern on remaining 15 sts until band fits halfway across back neck.

Cast off.

RIGHT FRONT

Work from ** to ** as given for left front.

Place pocket lining: Next row: Pattern 8 (12) (16) (20) (24), cast off 39 sts, pattern to end.

Next row: Pattern 16 (18) (20) (22) (24), pattern across 39 sts of pocket lining, pattern 8 (12) (16) (20) (24).

Pattern straight until front measures 76 (78) (80) (82) (84) cm from cast-on edge, ending with a right side row.

Shape upper arms and shoulders:
Cast off 8 (9) (10) (11) (12) sts at beginning of next and 5 following wrong side rows – 15 sts.

Continue in pattern on remaining 15 sts until band fits halfway across back neck.

Cast off.

To make up

Join shoulder and upper arm seams. Join cast-off edges of bands together; sew to back neck. Sew down pocket linings. Leaving 22 (23) (24) (25) (26) cm open for armhole and 15cm at lower side seam for split, join remaining side seams. Weave in all ends.

Clothing

Tip
If you don't have a stitchmarker big enough, cut a 4cm (2in) length of yarn in a contrasting colour, tie into a loose loop and thread onto needle.

What you need

1 x 160m (174yd) Rowan Big Wool super chunky yarn in:
- Carnival shade
- 10mm (US 15) circular needle, 40cm (16in) long
- Stitch marker
- Tapestry needle

FINISHED MEASUREMENTS
Circumference: 77.5cm (30.5in).
Height: 23.5cm (9in).

TENSION
89 sts and 12.5 rows = 10x10cm (4x4in) measured over st st using 10mm (US 15) needles, or the size required to obtain the correct tension.

ABBREVIATIONS
K, knit; **p**, purl; **st(s)**, stitch(es); **yo**, yarn over; **k2tog**, k 2 sts together (to decrease 1 st)

Cosy cowl

This pattern is perfect if you want to knit something cosy, but vibrant and colourful

Using 10mm (US 15) circular needle cast on 70 sts.
Being careful not to twist the cast on stitches, place a stitch marker and join to work in rnds as follows:
Rnd 1: Knit the first row.
Rnd 2: Purl.
Rnd 3: Knit.
Rnd 4: Purl.
Knit 4 rounds.
**Rnd 9: Purl.
Rnd 10: (yo, k2tog) to end of round.
Rnd 11: Purl.
Knit 4 rounds. **
Rep rnds 9 to 15 twice more.
Rnd 30: Purl.
Rnd 31: Knit.
Rnd 32: Purl.
Cast off kwise (knitting the sts).

To make up

Darn in ends. If you prefer, you can block the item, but it isn't necessary.

Clothing | 33

Ribbed scarf

This quick-to-knit scarf will keep anyone cosy, as the 2x3 rib stitch causes ripples in the fabric, which will hold in warm air

What you need

1 x 420m (459yd) Sirdar Hayfield Bonus Aran in:
- Denim
- 15mm (US 8) needles
- Tapestry needle

FINISHED MEASUREMENTS
140cm (55in) x 18cm (7in).

TENSION
28sts and 22 rows = 10cm (4in) in 2x3 rib stitch using 5mm (US 8) needles.

ABBREVIATIONS
K, knit; **p**, purl; **st(s)**, stitch(es)

Cast on 50 sts using 5mm needles
Row 1: *K3, P2; rep from * to end.
Row 2: *K2, P2; rep from * to end.

These 2 rows form 2x3 rib pattern. Continue in pattern until your knitting measures 140cm (55in), or your desired length, from the cast (bind) on edge.
Cast (bind) off.

To make up

Darn in ends and gently block.

Tip

You can use different combinations of knit and purl stitches to create a different looking rib pattern. A 2x2 rib is common for a good stretchy cuff on knitted hats.

Weekender hat

Knit in rounds to discover this easy, casual, yet elegant style – perfect for protecting against cold weather

What you need

1 (1) (1) x Rowan Cocoon yarn 80 per cent Merino, 20 per cent Kid Mohair (Ball)

- 1 stitch marker
- Tapestry needle

TENSION

14 sts and 20 rows = 10cm (4in) in stocking (stockinette) stitch using 6mm (US 10) needles.

ABBREVIATIONS

St(s), stitch(es); **k**, knit; **p**, purl; **k2tog**, knit 2 together; **yo**, yarn over; **ssk**, slip slip knit

Size		S	M	L
To fit size	cm in	18 45¾	21 53½	23 58½
Finished size	cm in	37 14¾	43 17¼	49.25 19¾

Yarn: Rowan Cocoon yarn 80 per cent Merino, 20 per cent Kid Mohair (Ball)			
Yarn A	1	1	1

Using 5.5mm needles and alternate cable cast-on method, cast (bind) on 48 (56, 64) sts.

Join in the round, being careful not to twist sts.

Place stitch marker to indicate start of round.

BRIM

Rnd 1: *K1, P1; rep from * to end.
Repeat this round for 5cm (2in) (or desired length).
Inc Rnd: *K2, M1; rep from * to end. (72, 84, 96 sts.)

NOTE ------------------

Pattern recommends the Alternate Cable cast-on method – any suitable rib cast-on method will work.

BODY

Change to 6mm (US 10) needles for the remainder of the hat, changing to the DPNs for the crown when the hat becomes too small to work comfortably on the circular needle.
Rnd 1: *Yo, K2tog; rep from * to end.
Repeat this round to form the bias eyelet rib pattern until the body of the hat (excluding the brim) measures 9.5 (10.25, 10.75) cm, 3.75 (4, 4.25) in.

CROWN

Foundation Rnd: Knit all sts.
45.75cm (18in) size jump to Rnd 5, 53.5cm (21in) size jump to Rnd 3, 58.5cm (23in) size start at Rnd 1, decreasing on every round as follows:
Rnd 1: *K14, ssk; rep from * to end. (90 sts.)
Rnd 2: *K13, ssk; rep from * to end. (84 sts.)
Rnd 3: *K12, ssk; rep from * to end. (78 sts.)
Rnd 4: *K11, ssk; rep from * to end. (72 sts.)
Rnd 5: *K10, ssk; rep from * to end. (66 sts.)
Rnd 6: *K9, ssk; rep from * to end. (60 sts.)
Rnd 7: *K8, ssk; rep from * to end. (54 sts.)
Rnd 8: *K7, ssk; rep from * to end. (48 sts.)
Rnd 9: *K6, ssk; rep from * to end. (42 sts.)
Rnd 10: *K5, ssk; rep from * to end. (36 sts.)
Rnd 11: *K4, ssk; rep from * to end. (30 sts.)
Rnd 12: *K3, ssk; rep from * to end. (24 sts.)
Rnd 13: *K2, ssk; rep from * to end. (18 sts.)
Rnd 14: *K1, ssk; rep from * to end. (12 sts.)
Rnd 15: *Ssk; rep from * to end. (6 sts.)

Break yarn and draw through remaining 6 sts. Tighten to close.

To make up

Weave in all ends. A gentle wash and blocking is required to help the decrease lines settle in and lay flat.

Clothing | 35

Pattern by Woolly Wormhead
Woolly is a Hat Architect. With a flair for unusual construction whose patterns are celebrated all over the world.
www.woollywormhead.com

Cotton top

Embellish this simple cotton top with running stitches for a pretty finish

What you need

10 (11) (12) (13) (14) x Sirdar Snuggly 100% Cotton DK (761) balls in:
- Cream (761)
- Teal (Spearmint 767)
- Pair each of 3.75mm (No. 9) knitting needles
- 4mm (No. 8) knitting needles
- Stitch holders
- Wool needle

TENSION

22 stitches and 28 rows, to 10 x 10cm, over stocking stitch, using 4mm needles.

ABBREVIATIONS

St(s), stitch(es); **k**, knit; **p**, purl; **sl**, slip; **tog**, together; **p2togb**, p2tog through back of sts; **inc**, increase (k into front then back of same st); **dec**, decrease (by taking 2 sts tog); **ss**, stocking st (k on right side and p on wrong side); **skpo**, (sl1, k1, pass sl st over); **nil**, meaning nothing is worked here for this size

NOTE

Yarn amounts are based on average requirements and are therefore approximate. Instructions are given for small size. Where they vary, work figures in round brackets for larger sizes. Instructions in square brackets are worked as stated after 2nd bracket.

Clothing 37

Size		S	M	L	XL	XXL
To fit size	cm	81	86	91	97	102
	in	32	34	36	38	40
Actual measurements	cm	86	91	97	101	107
	in	34	36	38	39¾	42
Side seam	cm	32	32	33	33.5	34
	in	12½	12½	13	13¼	13½
Length to back neck	cm	51.5	52	53	54	55
	in	20¼	20¼	21	21¼	21¾
Sleeve seam	cm	All sizes 44cm/17¼in.				
	in					

Yarn: Sirdar Snuggly 100% Cotton DK (761) ball(s)					
Yarn A Cream (761)	10	11	12	13	14
Yarn B Spearmint (767)	1	1	1	1	1

BACK

With 4mm needles and Cream, cast on 83 (89) (95) (101) (107) sts.
1st row: K40 (43) (46) (49) (52), p1, k1, p1, k40 (43) (46) (49) (52).
2nd row: P.
These 2 rows form pattern. Pattern another 14 rows.
Shape sides: Decrease row: K2, k2tog, pattern to last 4 sts, skpo, k2 – 2 sts decreased.
Pattern 7 rows, then repeat decrease row again – 79 (85) (91) (97) (103) sts.
Pattern 7 rows.
Increase row: K2, inc in next st, pattern to last 3 sts, inc in next st, k2 – 2 sts increased.
Pattern 5 rows.
Repeat last 6 rows, 6 (6) (6) (5) (5) times more, then work increase row again – 95 (101) (107) (111) (117) sts.
Pattern another 15 (15) (17) (25) (27) rows.
Shape raglan armholes:
1st row: Cast off 3 (4) (5) (5) (6) sts, (1 st on needle), p1, k1, k2tog, pattern to last 8 (9) (10) (10) (11) sts, skpo, k1, p1, k4 (5) (6) (6) (7).
2nd row: Cast off 3 (4) (5) (5) (6) sts, p to end – 87 (91) (95) (99) (103) sts.
3rd row: K1, p1, k1, k2tog, pattern to last 5 sts, skpo,
k1, p1, k1 – 2 sts decreased.
4th row: P.
5th row: K1, p1, pattern to last 2 sts, p1, k1.
6th row: P.
Repeat 3rd to 6th rows, 2 (2) (1) (1) (nil) time(s) more – 81 (85) (91) (95) (101) sts.
Next row: K1, p1, k1, k2tog, pattern to last 5 sts, skpo, k1, p1, k1 – 2 sts decreased.
Next row: P. **
Repeat last 2 rows, 19 (20) (22) (23) (25) times more – 41 (43) (45) (47) (49) sts.
Leave these sts on a st holder.

FRONT

Work as given for back to **.
Repeat last 2 rows, 11 (12) (14) (15) (17) times more – 57 (59) (61) (63) (65) sts.
Shape neck: Next row: K1, p1, k1, k2tog, k12, turn and work on these 16 sts for left side neck.
Left side neck: 1st row: P.
2nd row: K1, p1, k1, k2tog, k to last 2 sts, skpo – 2 sts decreased.
Repeat last 2 rows, 4 times more – 6 sts.
P 1 row. Leave these sts on a st holder.

Right side neck: With right side facing, slip centre 23 (25) (27) (29) (31) sts onto st holder, rejoin yarn to remaining sts, k12, skpo, k1, p1, k1 – 16 sts.
Next row: P.
Next row: K2tog, k to last 5 sts, skpo, k1, p1, k1.
Repeat last 2 rows, 4 times more – 6 sts.
P 1 row. Leave these sts on a st holder.

LEFT SLEEVE

With 4mm needles and Cream, cast on 43 (45) (47) (49) (51) sts.
1st row: K20 (21) (22) (23) (24), p1, k1, p1, k20 (21) (22) (23) (24).
2nd row: P.
These 2 rows form pattern. Pattern another 22 (22) (16) (16) (10) rows.
Increase row: K1, inc in next st, pattern to last 3 sts, inc in next st, k2 – 2 sts increased.
Pattern 5 rows.
Repeat last 6 rows, 11 (12) (13) (14) (15) times more, then work increase row again – 69 (73) (77) (81) (85) sts.
Pattern another 27 (21) (21) (15) (15) rows.
Shape raglan top: 1st row: Cast off 3 (4) (5) (5) (6) sts, k1 st more, p1, k1, k2tog, pattern to last 9 (10) (11) (11) (12) sts, skpo, k1, p1, k5 (6) (7) (7) (8).
2nd row: Cast off 3 (4) (5) (5) (6) sts, p to end – 61 (63) (65) (69) (71) sts.
3rd row: K2, p1, k1, k2tog, pattern to last 6 sts, skpo, k1, p1, k2 – 2 st decreased.
4th row: P.
5th row: K2, p1, pattern to last 3 sts, p1, k2.
6th row: P.
Repeat 3rd to 6th rows, 3 (3) (2) (1) (nil) time(s) more – 53 (55) (59) (65) (69) sts.
Next row: K2, p1, k1, k2tog, pattern to last 6 sts, skpo, k1, p1, k2 – 2 sts decreased.
Next row: P.
Repeat last 2 rows, 14 (15) (17) (20) (22) times more, then work first of the 2

rows again – 21 sts. ***
Shape neck: 1st row (wrong side): Cast off 2 sts, p to end – 19 sts.
2nd row: K2, p1, k1, k2tog, pattern 9, skpo, k2 – 17 sts.
3rd row: Cast off 4 sts, p to end – 13 sts.
4th row: K2, p1, k1, k2tog, pattern to end – 12 sts.
P 1 row. Leave these sts on a st holder

RIGHT SLEEVE

Work as given for left sleeve to ***.
P 1 row.
Shape neck: 1st row: Cast off 2 sts, k1 st more, k2tog, pattern 9, skpo, k1, p1, k2 – 17 sts. 2nd row: P.
3rd row: Cast off 4 sts, pattern to last 6 sts, skpo, k1, p1, k2 – 12 sts. 4th row: P.
Leave these sts on a st holder.

NECKBAND

Taking 1 st into the seam from each side, join both front and right back raglan seams. With right side facing and using 3.75mm needles, rejoin yarn to top of left sleeve,
k2, p1, k1, k2tog, [k1, p1] twice, skpo across sts on st holder, then pick up and k5
sts from neck shaping of left sleeve, p2tog, k1, skpo, k1 across sts on left side neck holder, then pick up and k6 sts down left front neck shaping, skpo, pattern 19 (21) (23)
(25) (27), k2tog across sts at centre front, pick up and k6 sts up right front neck shaping, then k1, k2tog, k1, p2togb across sts on right side neck holder, pick up and k5 sts
from neck shaping of right sleeve, then k2tog, [p1, k1] twice, k1, skpo, k1, k2tog across sts on st holder, finally, p2tog, [k1, k2tog] twice, pattern 25 (27) (29) (31) (33), [skpo, k1] twice, p1, k1 across back neck sts – 106 (110) (114) (118) (122) sts.
Beginning with a p row, work 7 rows in ss.
Cast off knitwise.

To make up

Join left back raglan seam, including neckband.
With right side facing and using blunt-ended wool needle, run a single thread of Teal under each line of purl sts to resemble top-stitching, making sure that threads do not pull in the fabric, securing at each end. Taking 1 st into seam, join side and sleeve seams.

Clothing | 39

Lace shawl

A beautiful look to create using this easy-to-follow pattern, this lace shawl could make for the perfect personal present

What you need

1 x 365m (400yd) 3 or 4-ply Claudia's Hand Painted Yarn in:
- Mudslide
- 4mm (US 6) 91cm/36in circular needle
- 2 stitch markers (Marker 1)
- 26 stitch markers in a different colour or style (Marker 2)
- Tapestry needle

FINISHED MEASUREMENTS
Width: 183cm (72in) after blocking
Depth: 33cm (13in) after blocking.

TENSION
18sts and 28 rows = 10cm (4in) in horseshoe lace stitch using 4mm needles after blocking.

ABBREVIATIONS
K, knit; **p**, purl; **st(s)**, stitch(es); **yo**, yarn over; **sl**, slip; **pm**, place marker; **k2tog**, k 2 sts together (to decrease 1 st); **psso**, pass slip st over; **ssk**, slip slip knit

Cast (bind) on 277 sts, placing the sts markers as follows:
Cast (bind) on 3, PM1, (cast (bind) on 10 sts, PM1) 12 times, (cast (bind) on 10 sts, PM2) twice, (cast (bind) on 10 sts, PM1) 13 times, cast (bind) on 4.

The first part of the shawl is worked in garter st (knit every row), but with short rows to give it a curved shape. When working short rows in garter st it is not necessary to wrap the sts to prevent holes.

The stitch markers you have added to the cast (bind) on row help you keep count when casting (binding) on, mark where you will be turning on the short rows and highlight the central 10 sts. They will also serve to mark the placing of repeats of the lace charts later on in the pattern.

SECTION 1
Row 1: Knit until you reach the furthest marker. With the marker still on the LH needle, turn your work around ready to knit back the other way.
Next row: As row 1.
Row 3: Knit until you reach the next marker in from the one that you previously turned at. With the marker still on the LH needle, turn.
Repeat row 3, turning one marker in from the previous one on every row until you reach the middle 20 sts of the shawl. Turn.
Next row: Knit to end of row, turn. Knit back across all the sts.
This is the first set of short row shaping complete.

NOTE
Using a lace cast (bind) off is best as it is stretchy and will allow you to block the shawl to open the lace up and show it off.

SECTION 2
Row 1: Knit across the sts until you reach the 4th marker from the end of the row. With the marker still on the LH needle, turn your work around ready to knit back the other way.
Row 2: Repeat row 1.
Row 3: Knit across the sts until you reach the next marker in from the one that you previously turned at. With the marker still on the RH needle, turn your work around ready to knit back the other way.
Continue to work in short rows, turning one marker in from the previous row until you have worked only the 10 sts between the 2 markers at the middle of the row. Turn.
Next row: Knit to end of row, turn. Knit back across all the sts. This is the second set of short row shaping completed.

LACE SECTION
Work rows 1-8 of the Lace Pattern chart, repeating the 10 sts within the red border 27 times in all.
Rep these 8 rows a further 4 times. Work rows 1-8, 5 times in all.
Work rows 1-6 of the Lace Border chart, repeating the 10 sts within the red border 27 times in all. Work rows 1-6 once.
Cast (bind) off all sts using a lace cast (bind) off.

Lace border

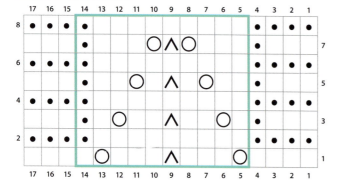

Lace shawl

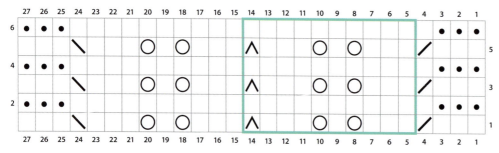

Key: ☐ = knit   ● = purl   ○ = yo   ╱ = RS: k2tog / WS: p2tog   ╲ = RS: ssk / WS: p2tog tbl   ∧ = sl1, k2tog, psso   ☐ = name of repeat

LACE CAST (BIND) OFF

K2 sts, slip sts back onto LH needle, *k2tog tbl, K1, sl sts back onto LH needle* rep from * to end. Cut yarn, slip end through the last st and tighten.

To make up

Soak the shawl in a wool wash and rinse. Squeeze out as much water as possible, wrap in a towel and press hard to remove more without agitating, which can cause the yarn to felt. Pin out the damp shawl on a flat surface to the shape and dimensions given in the schematic. Pin out the points of each repeat. Leave until dry, unpin and sew in any ends.

NOTE

A crescent-shaped shawl that is constructed using short rows on a garter stitch base. The beauty of these is that you do not need to wrap the stitches to avoid gaps. The shawl is finished off with a deep edging of horseshoe lace, a traditional Shetland stitch pattern.

Prefer it written?

If you find charts difficult to work with, don't despair. Many designers usually provide written versions of stitch patterns for those knitters who prefer to use them. If not it is very easy to create your own. All you need to do is to write down the sts in each row, remembering to read RS rows from right to left, and WS rows from left to right.

LACE PATTERN CHART
(WRITTEN VERSION)

Row 1 (RS): K4, *yo, K3, sl1, k2tog, psso, K3, yo, K1; rep from * to last 3 sts, K3.
Row 2 (WS): *K1, P9; rep from * to last 4 sts, K4.
Row 3 (RS): K3, P1, (K1, yo, K2, sl1, k2tog, psso, K2, yo, K1, P1) repeat 27 times in all, K3.
Row 4 (WS): As row 2.
Row 5 (RS): K3, P1, (K2, yo, K1, sl1, k2tog, psso, K1, yo, K2, P1) repeat 27 times in all, K3.
Row 6 (WS): As row 2.
Row 7 (RS): K3, P1, (K3, yo, sl1, k2tog, psso, yo, K3, P1) repeat 27 times in all, K3.
Row 8 (WS): As row 2.

LACE BORDER CHART
(WRITTEN VERSION)

Row 1 (RS): K3, k2tog, *K3, yo, K1, yo, K3, sl1, k2tog, psso; rep from * to last 12 sts, K3, yo, K1, yo, K3, ssk, K3.
Row 2 (WS): K3, P to last 3 sts, K3.
Row 3 (RS): As row 1.
Row 4 (WS): As row 2.
Row 5 (RS): As row 1.
Row 6 (WS): K3, P to last 3 sts, K3.

Pattern by Janine Le Cras
Janine is a lifelong knitter who learned to knit at her grandmother's knee. After a break she discovered the world of knitting on the web, which had a new and vibrant image, and was re-inspired to pick up her needles.

Pattern by Lynne Rowe
Lynne Rowe is a knit and crochet designer, technical editor, craft author and tutor. She loves to pass on her skills to help others to knit, crochet and create.
www.thewoolnest.blogspot.co.uk
& www.knitcrochetcreate.com

Clothing

Chunky ribbed hat

Add a fluffy pom pom to a classic ribbed hat to create a fun and quick-to-make accessory

What you need

1 x 100g (134m) King Cole Riot Chunky 70% acrylic, 30% wool in:
- Rhinestone colour

Or another equivalent Chunky weight yarn
- 5.5mm circular needle, 50cm (20in) long
- 6mm circular needles, 50cm (20in) long
- 6mm DPNS
- Stitch markers
- Yarn needle

TENSION

14 sts and 20 rows = 10cm (4in) over stocking stitch using 6mm needles.

ABBREVIATIONS

K, knit; **p**, purl; **k2tog**, k 2 sts together (to decrease 1 st); **p2tog**, purl 2 stitches together

Size		S	M	L
To fit adult head (stretches to fit head)	cm	53.4	56	58.5

MAIN HAT

Using 6mm circular needle and col 1, cast on 72[80 : 88]sts.
Join in the rnd ready to start knitting (taking care not to twist the stitches) and place a stitch marker before the first stitch. Slip the stitch marker after each rnd.
Rnd 1: *K2, P2; rep from * to end.
Rnd 1 forms rib. Cont in rib until hat measures approx 7cm from the start.
Change to 5.5mm circular needle. Cont in rib until hat measures approx 14 cm from the start. Mark the last rnd with a stitch marker or a piece of waste yarn.
Change to 6mm circular needles. Cont in rib until hat measures approximately 25[25 : 27.5]cm from the start.

SHAPE CROWN

NOTE: change to 6mm dpns when you have too few stitches to work comfortably on your circular needle.
Rnd 1: *K2, p2tog, K2, P2; rep from * to end. (63[70 : 77]sts)
Rnd 2: *K2, P1, K2, P2; rep from * to end. (63[70 : 77]sts)
Rnd 3: *K2, P1, K2, p2tog; rep from * to end. (54[60 : 66]sts)
Rnd 4: *K2, P1; rep from * to end. (54[60 : 66]sts)
Rnd 5: *K2tog, P1, K2, P1; rep from * to

end. (45[50 : 55]sts)
Rnd 6: *K1, P1, K2, P1); rep from * to end. (45[50 : 55]sts)
Rnd 7: *K1, P1, k2tog, P1; rep from * to end. (36[40: 44]sts)
Rnd 8: *K1, P1; rep from * to end. (36[40 : 44]sts)
Rnd 9: *K2tog; rep from * to end. (18[20 : 22]sts)
Rnd 10: *K2tog; rep from * to end. (9[10 : 11]sts)

To make up

Cut yarn, leaving a long tail. Thread tail onto yarn needle and thread it through the remaining 9[10 : 11]sts, taking them off the needle. Pull tight to gather and fasten off securely. Weave any yarn ends into WS and trim.

Turn hat to right side. If desired, make a large pompom and attached to the hat.

Fold up brim to the marked round and remove marker. If desired, secure the fold with a few stitches.

NOTE

Slightly more stitches are used that tension suggests, due using a rib pattern.

Clothing | 45

Gradient shawl

This stylish, asymmetric shawl is easy to wear and knit, and is great for showcasing beautiful gradient yarns

What you need

1 x 100g (365m) Dyeninja High Twist Merino Fingering in:
- Limestone

1 x 100g (400m) Bilum Slika hand dyed gradient 4 ply in:
- Yellow to Blue gradient
- 3.75mm circular needle, 80cm (32in) long
- Yarn needle

FINISHED MEASUREMENTS

230cm (90½in) wide and 55cm (21¾in) deep after blocking. Final measurements will vary depending on how aggressively the shawl is blocked.

TENSION

Work 24 sts and 34 rows in stocking stitch to measure 10x10cm/4x4in before blocking, using 3.75mm (US 5) needles, or size required to obtain correct tension.

ABBREVIATIONS

St(s), stitch(es); **k**, knit; **p**, purl; **gst**, garter stitch (every row k); **inc**, increase 1 st (by working into back and front of the same st); **dec**, decrease 1 st, by working k2tog on a k row and p2tog on a p row; **ss**, stocking st (k on right side and p on wrong side); **tog**, together

Using 3.75mm circular needle and col 1, cast on 4 sts.
Row 1 (RS): Sl 1 wyib, Kfb, knit to end. (5 sts).
Row 2 (WS): Sl 1 wyib, K2tog, knit to last st, Kfb. (5 sts).
Rows 1 & 2 set gst pattern, with increases and decrease at edges, and all gst pattern rows will be worked in this way throughout the rest of the piece.
Rows 3-32: Cont to shape edges as set, work a further 30 rows in gst pattern. (20 sts).
Change to col 2.
Row 33: Sl 1 wyib, Kfb, knit to end. (21 sts).
Row 34: Sl 1 wyif, P2tog, purl to last st, Pfb. (21 sts).
These 2 rows set st-st pattern, with increases and decrease at edges, and all st-st pattern rows will be worked in this way throughout the rest of the piece.
Rows 35-52: Cont to shape edges as set, work a further 18 rows in st-st pattern. (30 sts).
Change to col 1.
Rows 53-54: Cont to shape edges as set, work 2 rows in gst pattern. (31 sts)
Row 55 (eyelet row): Sl 1 wyib, yfwd, K1, *yfwd, K2tog; rep from * to last st, K1.

Tip

When you finish each row, check the ends to ensure you have increased or decreased correctly, as it can be easy to lose track and will save you a lot of time undoing any mistakes if found later, particularly when your rows get very long towards the end of the project.

(32 sts).
Row 56: Sl 1 wyib, K2tog, K to last st, Kfb. (32 sts).
Change to col 2.
Rows 57-76: Beg with a knit row and cont to shape edges as set, work 20 rows in st-st pattern. (42 sts).
Change to col 1.
Rows 77-80: Cont to shape edges as set, work 4 rows in gst pattern. (44 sts).
Row 81 (eyelet row): Sl 1 wyib, yfwd, K1, *yfwd, K2tog; rep from * to end. (45 sts).
Rows 82-84: Cont to shape edges as set, work 3 rows in gst pattern. (46 sts).
Change to col 2.
Rows 85-102: Beg with a knit row and cont to shape edges as set, work 18 rows in st-st pattern. (55 sts).
Change to col 1.
Rows 103-104: Cont to shape edges as set, work 2 rows in gst pattern. (56 sts).

NOTE

The shawl is knitted flat, but a circular needle is used to accommodate the large number of stitches that there will be at the cast off edge.
Shaping is worked at the edges of every row, and the number of stitches will increase by 1 stitch for every 2 rows worked.

Quick & Easy KNITTING

Row 105 (eyelet row): Sl 1 wyib, yfwd, K1, *yfwd, K2tog; rep from * to end. (57 sts).
Row 106: Sl 1 wyib, K2tog, knit to last st, Kfb. (57 sts).
Change to col 2.
Rows 107-124: Beg with a knit row and cont to shape edges as set, work 18 rows in st st pattern. (66 sts).
Change to col 1.
Rows 125-128: Cont to shape edges as set, work 4 rows in gst pattern. (68 sts).
Row 129 (eyelet row): Sl 1 wyib, yfwd, K1, *yfwd, K2tog; rep from * to end. (69 sts).
Rows 130-132: Cont to shape edges as set, work 3 rows in gst pattern. (70 sts).
Change to col 2.
Rows 133-148: Beg with a knit row and cont to shape edges as set, work 16 rows in st-st pattern. (78 sts).
Change to col 1.
Rows 149-158: Cont to shape edges as set, work 10 rows in gst pattern. (83 sts).
Change to col 2.
Rows 159-174: Beg with a knit row and cont to shape edges as set, work 16 rows in st-st pattern. (91 sts).
Change to col 1.
Rows 175-178: Cont to shape edges as set, work 4 rows in gst pattern. (93 sts).
Row 179 (eyelet row): Sl 1 wyib, yfwd, K1, *yfwd, K2tog; rep from * to last st, K1. (94 sts).
Rows 180-182: Cont to shape edges as set, work 3 rows in gst pattern. (95 sts).
Change to col 2.
Rows 183-202: Beg with a knit row and cont to shape edges as set, work 20 rows in st-st pattern. (105 sts).
Change to col 1.
Rows 203-204: Cont to shape edges as set, work 2 rows in gst pattern. (106 sts).
Row 205 (eyelet row): Sl 1 wyib, yfwd, K1, *yfwd, K2tog; rep from * to end. (107 sts).
Row 206: Sl 1 wyib, K2tog, knit to last st, Kfb. (107 sts).
Change to col 2.
Rows 207-228: Beg with a knit row and cont to shape edges as set, work 22 rows in st-st pattern. (118 sts).
Change to col 1.
Rows 229-232: Cont to shape edges as set, work 4 rows in gst pattern. (120 sts).
Row 233 (eyelet row): Sl 1 wyib, yfwd, K1, *yfwd, K2tog; rep from * end. (121 sts).
Rows 234-236: Cont to shape edges as set, work 3 rows in gst pattern. (122 sts).
Change to col 2.
Rows 237-260: Beg with a knit row and cont to shape edges as set, work 24 rows in st-st pattern. (134 sts).
Change to col 1.
Rows 261-276: Cont to shape edges as set, work 16 rows in gst pattern. (142 sts).
Change to col 2.
Rows 277-310: Beg with a knit row and cont to shape edges as set, work 34 rows in st-st pattern. (159 sts).
Change to col 1.
Rows 311-314: Cont to shape edges as set, work 4 rows in gst pattern. (161 sts).
Row 315 (eyelet row): Sl 1 wyib, yfwd, K1, *yfwd, K2tog; rep from * to last st, K1. (162 sts).
Rows 316-322: Cont to shape edges as set, work 7 rows in gst pattern. (165 sts).
Row 323 (eyelet row): Sl 1 wyib, yfwd, K1, *yfwd, K2tog; rep from * to last st, K1. (166 sts).
Rows 324-326: Cont to shape edges as set, work 3 rows in gst pattern. (167 sts)

Change to col 2.
Rows 327-364: Beg with a knit row and cont to shape edges as set, work 38 rows in st-st pattern. (186 sts).

NOTE: If desired you can continue working in col 2 at this point, until your yarn runs out, ending with a WS row.

Change to col 1.
Rows 365-412: Cont to shape edges as set, work 48 rows in gst pattern. (210 sts).
Row 413 (eyelet row): Sl 1 wyib, yfwd, K1, *yfwd, K2tog; rep from * to end. (211 sts).
Rows 414-416: Cont to shape edges as set, work 3 rows in gst pattern. (212 sts). Cast off knit-wise for a plain edge if preferred or work picot cast off as follows:
Picot cast-off: cast off 2 sts, *transfer stitch on right-hand needle back into left-hand needle, cast on 2 sts, cast off 4 sts; rep from * to end, fasten off.

To make up

Sew in all ends on wrong side. Blocking is easy and will dramatically improve the appearance of your shawl and should not be skipped. Block by first soaking and gently squeezing excess water out. Alternatively spray liberally with cool water, patting the water into the knitting until thoroughly wet then pin out flat to dimensions given - the longest edge will be gently curved, and the other two edges will be straight. Leave to try dry completely before unpinning - this may take a few days but be patient or it won't be fully blocked.

Quick & Easy KNITTING

Hat & wrist-warmers

This gorgeous set is soft and cosy, and it's simple to make; beginners will particularly love the wrist-warmers

Beret

With 3.25mm needles,
cast on 86 sts.
Beginning with a k row, ss 8 rows.
Change to 4mm needles.
P 1 row.
1st increase row: K4, [inc
in next st, k6] 11 times,
inc in next st, k4 – 98 sts.
P 1 row.
2nd increase row: K1, inc in next st, [k6,
inc in each of next 2 sts] 11 times, k6,
inc in next st, k1 – 122 sts.
P1 row.
3rd increase row: K1, inc
in next st, [k8, inc in each
of next 2 sts] 11 times, k8,
in next st, k1 – 146 sts.
K 1 row and p 1 row.
4th increase row: K1, inc
in next st, [k10, inc in each
of next 2 sts] 11 times, k10, inc in next st,
k1 – 170 sts.
P1 row, k 1 row and p 1 row.
Beginning with p row, rss

6 rows.
Beginning with a k row, ss
6 rows.
Last 12 rows form pattern.
Pattern another 42 rows.

SHAPE CROWN

1st decrease row: K2, [k2tog, k9, skpo,
k1] 12 times – 146 sts.
Pattern 6 rows.
2nd decrease row: [Skpo,
k1, k2tog, k7] 12 times,
k2 – 122 sts. Pattern 4 rows.
3rd decrease row: K2, [k2tog, k5, skpo,
k1] 12 times – 98 sts.
Pattern 6 rows.
4th decrease row: [Skpo, k1, k2tog, k3]
12 times, k2 – 74 sts.
Pattern 4 rows.
5th decrease row: K2, [k2tog, k1, skpo,
k1] 12 times – 50 sts.
Pattern 6 rows.
6th decrease row: [K1, s2kpo] 12 times,
k2 – 26 sts.
P 1 row.

7th decrease row: [S2kpo]
8 times, k2 – 10 sts.
Break off yarn, leaving a
long end. Thread end through
remaining sts, draw up tightly and
secure. Join back seam, reversing
seam on first 6 rows for edge.

Wrist-warmers (make two)

With 4mm needles, cast on 44 sts for
top edge.
Beginning with a k row, ss 8 rows.
Beginning with a p row, rss – 6 rows.
Beginning with a k row, ss 6 rows.
The last 12 rows form pattern.
Pattern another 12 rows.
Change to 3.25mm needles.
Pattern another 24 rows.
Change to 4mm needles.
Pattern another 30 rows.
Cast off.
Leaving an opening for thumb, join
seam, reversing seam on first 8 rows
for rolled edge.

Clothing 49

What you need

FOR BERET
4 x 50g (140m) balls of King Cole Luxury Merino DK (100% merino wool) in:
- Snowy Sky (2626)*

FOR WRIST-WARMERS
3 x 50g (140m) balls of King Cole Luxury Merino DK (100% merino wool) in:
- Snowy Sky (2626)*

FOR BOTH
- Pair each of 3.25mm (No. 10) and 4mm (No. 8) knitting needles

TENSION
22 stitches and 36 rows, to 10 x 10cm, over pattern, using 4mm needles.

ABBREVIATIONS
K, knit; **p**, purl; **st(s)**, stitch(es); **tog**, together; **inc**, increase (by working twice into same st); **dec**, decrease (by taking 2 sts tog); **ss**, stocking st (k on right side, p on wrong side); **rss**, reverse ss (p on right side, k on wrong side); **skpo**, slip 1, k1, pass slip st over; **s2kpo**, slip next 2 sts as if about to k2tog, k1, pass 2 slip sts over

Fingerless mitts

Sometimes fingered gloves just aren't practical, so who not have a go at making these funky fingerless mitts?

What you need

1 (1) (1) x 4 ply yarn Wendy Roam Fusion in:
- Force (above)
- Heath (right)
- 2¾ mm (US 2) knitting needles

TENSION
37 sts and 52 rows = 10 cm (4 ins) over basket weave stitch.

ABBREVIATIONS
St(s), stitch(es); **k**, knit; **p**, purl; **patt**, pattern

Size	S	M	L
cm	15	18	19
in	6	7	7½

NOTE

There is a lot of counting involved in the pattern. When reaching the thumb, remember to count the 35 stitches across before breaking the basket weave in order to do the thumb stitches.
Be wary when following the 'patt to end' in order to match it up to continue the basketweave effect.

Basketweave fingerless mitts

Using 2¾ mm needles, cast (bind) on 57 (65, 73) sts.

RIBBED CUFF

1st Row: K3, P2, * K2, P2 rep from * to end.
2nd Row: * K2, P2, rep from * to last st, P1
These two rows form rib. Continue in rib as set until work measures 7cm, 2¾ ins.

Commence basket weave pattern
Row 1: (rs) K1, * K2, P6, rep from * to end.
Row 2: (ws) * K6, P2, rep from * to last st, P1.

Row 3: As row 1.
Row 4: Purl.
Row 5: P5, * K2, P6, rep from * to last 4 stitches, K2, P2.
Row 6: K2, P2, *K6, P2, rep from * to last 5 sts, K5.
Row 7: As row 5.
Row 8: Purl.

These rows form basket weave pattern. Work rows 1 to 8 once and then work rows 1 to 4.

THUMB

Row 13: Keeping basket weave pattern correct, and starting from 5th row of pattern, patt 28 (32, 36) sts, M1, K2, M1, patt to end.
Row 14: Patt 27 (31, 35) sts, P4, patt to end.
Row 15: Patt 28 (32, 36) sts, K4, patt to end.
Row 16: Patt 27 (31, 35) sts, M1 pwise, P4, M1 pwise, patt to end.
Row 17: Patt 28 (32, 36) sts, K6, patt to end.
Row 18: Patt 27 (31, 35) sts, P6, patt to end.
Row 19: Patt 28 (32, 36) sts, M1, K6, M1, patt to end.
Row 20: Patt 27 (31, 35) sts, P8, patt to end.
Row 21: Patt 28 (32, 36) sts, K8, patt to end.
Row 22: Patt 27 (31, 35) sts, M1 pwise, P8, M1 pwise, patt to end.
Row 23: Patt 28 (32, 36) sts, K10, patt to end.
Row 24: Patt 27 (31, 35) sts, P10, patt to end.
Row 25: Patt 28 (32, 36) sts, M1, K10, M1, patt to end.
Row 26: Patt 27 (31, 35) sts, P12, patt to end.
Row 27: Patt 28 (32, 36) sts, K12, patt to end.
Row 28: Patt 27 (31, 35) sts, M1 pwise, P12, M1 pwise, patt to end.
Row 29: Patt 28 (32, 36) sts, K14, patt to end.
Row 30: Patt 27 (31, 35) sts, P14, patt to end.
Row 31: Patt 28 (32, 36) sts, M1, K14, M1, patt to end.
Row 32: Patt 27 (31, 35) sts, P16, patt to end.
Row 33: Patt 28 (32, 36) sts, K16, patt to end.
Row 34: Patt 27 (31, 35) sts, M1 pwise, P16, M1 pwise, patt to end.
Row 35: Patt 28 (32, 36) sts, K18, patt to end.
Row 36: Patt 27 (31, 35) sts, P18, patt to end.
Row 37: Patt 28 (32, 36) sts, M1, K18, M1, patt to end.
Row 38: Patt 27 (31, 35) sts, P20, patt to end.
Row 39: Patt 28 (32, 36) sts, K20, patt to end.

1ST SIZE ONLY

Row 40: Patt 27 (31, 35) sts, slip next 20 sts onto a safety pin, cast (bind) on 2 sts, patt to end.

2ND AND 3RD SIZES ONLY

Row 40: Patt (31, 35) sts, M1 pwise, P20, M1 pwise, patt to end.
Row 41: Patt (32, 36) sts, K22, patt to end.
Row 42: Patt (31, 35) sts, M1 pwise, P22, M1 pwise, patt to end.
Row 43: Patt (32, 36) sts, K 24, patt to end.
Row 44: Patt (31, 35) sts, slip next 24 sts onto a safety pin, cast (bind) on 2 sts, patt to end.

ALL SIZES

Work 16 (18, 20) more rows in basket weave pattern over all 57 (65, 73) sts on needle.
Work 8 rows in rib, as worked for ribbed cuff.
Cast (bind) off.

THUMB

Return to sts left on safety pin, rejoin yarn with wrong side facing and P across 20 (24, 24) sts, pick up and P 4 sts over the 2 cast (bind) on sts.

Next Row: K1, M1, K1, P2, * K2, P2, rep from * to end.
Next Row: * K2, P2, rep from * to last st, P1.
Next Row: K3, P2, *K2, P2, rep from * to end.

Rep last 2 rows 4 times more, and then cast (bind) off in rib.

To make up

Join side seam and thumb seam by top sewing.
Repeat for the other mitt.

Pattern by
Thomas B Ramsden
This pattern was kindly supplied by Thomas B Ramsden, a family business who are the suppliers of Wendys and Peter Pan, two of the biggest brands of yarn in the UK.
www.tbramsden.co.uk

Garter stitch scarf

Pick an interesting yarn with texture and colour variations in order to make a creative garter stitch scarf

What you need

1 x 135m (147yd) Sirdar Bohemia super chunky yarn in:
- Ombre
- plus more for tassels
- 15mm (US 19) needles
- Crochet hook for tassels

FINISHED MEASUREMENTS
152cm (60in).

TENSION
7 stitches and 10 rows = 10x10cm (4x4in) in garter stitch using 15mm (US 19) needles, or size required to obtain correct tension (gauge).

ABBREVIATIONS
K, knit; **st(s)**, stitches

Using 15mm needles, cast (bind) on 14 sts leaving a long tail.
Row 1: Knit.

Continue to knit every row until you have worked all three balls of yarn leaving enough to cast (bind) off or have a scarf the length that you require.
Add your new balls at the start of the row.
Cast (bind) off knitwise and cut the yarn leaving a long tail.

To make up

Darn in yarn tails, however if you are adding tassels to your scarf, there is no need to darn in the cast (bind) on and cast (bind) off tails of yarn.

MAKING TASSELS

1. Wind your yarn loosely around an object to obtain the length you require.

2. Cut the yarn along the bottom edge. You will now have lengths of yarn. Be careful to keep them all the same length.

3. Taking two strands of yarn, insert your crochet hook into the end of the scarf, catch the middle of the yarn on the hook and pull through the knitting to make a loop.

4. Feed the four yarn ends through the loop and pull tight. Repeat this to add more tassels at equal intervals along both ends of the scarf. Once you have added all the tassels, cut all to the same

NOTE
If you prefer a narrower scarf, cast (bind) on fewer stitches. Similarly, to make a wider scarf, cast (bind) on more stitches.

Staggered beanie

What you need

Debbie Bliss Blue Faces Leicester DK (see table for amount) in:

- Chestnut
- 3.25mm (US 3) circular needle, 40cm (16in) long
- 3.25mm (US 3) DPNs
- 1 stitch marker
- Tapestry needle

TENSION

22 sts and 35 rounds = 10cm (4in) in stocking (stockinette) stitch.

ABBREVIATIONS

St(s), stitch(es); **k**, knit; **p**, purl; **gst**, garter stitch (every row k); **tog**, together; **ssp**, slip slip purl

Create this fantastic beanie with a staggered block pattern by knitting in the round, perfect as a gift for anyone

Size		S	M	L	XL	XXL
To fit sizes	cm in	15 18	18 45¾	20 50¾	22 56	24 61
Finished size	cm in	13 33¼	15.25 38¾	17.5 44¼	19.75 50	21.75 55½

Yarn: Debbie Bliss Blue Faces Leicester DK yarn						
Chestnut	m yd	45 49	60 66	78 85	98 107	120 131

Using cast (bind) on method of your choice, cast (bind) on 72 (84, 96, 108, 120) sts onto the circular needle. Join in the round, being careful not to twist sts. Place stitch marker to indicate start of round.

BRIM

Rnd 1: *K3, P3; repeat from * to end
Repeat this round until brim measures 1 (1.25, 1.5, 1.75, 2) in/2.5 (3.25, 3.75, 4.5, 5) cm.

BODY

Rnd 1: *K3, P9; repeat from * to end

Repeat this round for a further 1 (1¼, 1½, 1¾, 2) in/2.5 (3.25, 3.75, 4.5, 5) cm until work measures 2 (2½, 3, 3½, 4) in/5 (6.25, 7.5, 9, 10.25) cm from cast (bind)-on edge. Work as follows:

Next rnd: Purl all sts

Repeat this round, forming reverse stocking (stockinette) stitch, for a further 1.5in/3.75cm until work measures 3.5 (4, 4½, 5, 5½) in/9 (10.25, 11.5, 12.75, 14) cm from cast (bind)-on edge.

CROWN PREPARATION

18in size only: *p2tog, P19; repeat from * to end. 80 sts.
22in size only: *P12, p2tog, P13; repeat from * to end. 104 sts.

CROWN

15in/38cm size jump to Rnd 13;
18in/45cm size jump to Rnd 11;
20in/50.75cm size jump to Rnd 7;
22in/56cm size jump to Rnd 5;
24in/61cm size start at Rnd 1.

As you work through these instructions, as the hat gets too small to work comfortably on the circular needle, change to DPNs.

Rnd 1: *(ssp, P26, p2tog); repeat from * to end. 112 sts.

Rnd 2 & all even rounds: Purl all sts
Rnd 3: P12, p2tog, (ssp, P24, p2tog) 3 times, ssp, P12. 104 sts.
Rnd 5: *(ssp, P22, p2tog); repeat from * to end. 96 sts.
Rnd 7: P10, p2tog, (ssp, P20, p2tog) 3 times, ssp, P10/ 88 sts.
Rnd 9: *(ssp, P18, p2tog); repeat from * to end. 80 sts.
Rnd 11: P8, p2tog, (ssp, P16, p2tog) 3 times, ssp, P8/ 72 sts.
Rnd 13: *(ssp, P14, p2tog); repeat from * to end. 64 sts.
Rnd 15: P6, p2tog, (ssp, P12, p2tog) 3 times, ssp, P6. 56 sts.
Rnd 17: *(ssp, P10, p2tog); repeat from * to end. 48 sts.
Rnd 19: P4, p2tog, (ssp, P8, p2tog) 3 times, ssp, P4. 40 sts.
Rnd 21: *(ssp, P6, p2tog); repeat from * to end. 32 sts.
Rnd 23: P2, p2tog, (ssp, P4, p2tog) 3 times, ssp, P2. 24 sts.
Rnd 25: *(ssp, P2, p2tog); repeat from * to end. 16 sts.
Rnd 27: *(p2tog, ssp); repeat from * to end.
8 sts.

Break yarn and draw through remaining 8 sts, tighten to close.

To make up

Weave in all ends. A gentle wash and blocking is required to help the decreases settle in and lay flat.

Pattern by
Woolly Wormhead
Woolly is a Hat Architect. With a flair for unusual construction whose patterns are celebrated all over the world.
www.woollywormhead.com

What you need

For this pattern you shall require 4 x 50g (200m) balls of Sirdar Country Classic 4 Ply (40% nylon, 30% wool, 30% acrylic) in each:
- Lime Green (Chartreuse 966)
- Navy (952)
- 3 balls in Red (True Red 971)*
- Pair of 2.75mm (No. 12) knitting needles
- Stitch holder

TENSION
34 stitches and 38 rows, to 10 x 10cm, over stocking stitch, using 2.75mm needles.

ABBREVIATIONS
St(s), stitch(es); **k**, knit; **p**, purl; **ss**, stocking st (k on the right side and p on the wrong side); **k2tog**, k 2 sts together (to decrease 1 st); **wrap 1 (on a k row)**, ytf, slip 1, ytb, place slipped st back on left-hand needle, on following k row, using right-hand needle, pick up the wrap and knit it together with the st above it; wrap 1 (on a p row), ytb, slip 1, ytf, place slipped st back on left-hand needle, on following p row, using right-hand needle, pick up the wrap and purl it together with the st above it; **ytf**, bring yarn to front of work; **ytb**, take yarn to back of work

Knitted socks

If you've not tried to knit socks before, this simple pattern is ideal for a first attempt!

Finished measurements	To fit an average man's foot
Length of foot from toe to back of heel	28.5cm/11¼in.
Ankle/leg circumference	23.5cm/9¼in.
Length from top of sock to base of heel	29cm/11½in..

Yarn: Sirdar Country Classic 4 Ply (40% nylon, 30% wool, 30% acrylic)	Ball(s)
Yarn A Lime Green (Chartreuse 966)	4
Yarn B Navy (952)	4
Yarn C Red (True Red 971)	3

Clothing 57

Plain-ish Socks

Striped Socks (both alike)

With 2.75mm needles and
Navy yarn, cast on 79 sts.
1st rib row: K1, [p1, k1] to end.
2nd rib row: P1, [k1, p1] to end. Last 2 rows form rib.
Rib another 8 rows. **
Join in Lime and beginning with a k row, ss 2 rows.
Ss another 64 rows, working in stripe sequence of 6 rows in
Red, 2 rows in Lime, 6 rows in Navy and 2 rows in Lime.
Continuing stripe sequence,
ss another 11 rows, ending with the 3rd Navy row and with wrong side facing.
Join in Lime at this edge, leaving Navy still attached.

DIVIDE FOR HEEL

1st row: P40 and turn.
* **2nd and 3rd rows:** K38, wrap 1, turn. P36, wrap 1, turn.
4th and 5th rows: K35, wrap 1, turn. P34, wrap 1, turn.
6th and 7th rows: K33 wrap 1, turn. P32, wrap 1, turn.
Work 18 rows more as set, working 1 st less before the
wrap on every row, ending with p14, wrap 1, turn.
26th and 27th rows: K14, wrap 1 (you will now have two wraps around this stitch), turn. P14, wrap 1 (you will now have two wraps around this stitch), turn.
28th row: K14, pick up the two wrapped loops of yarn from around the next stitch, place them on the left needle
and work them both together with the next stitch,
wrap 1, turn.
As you work over all of the following double-wrapped stitches, work each of them together with their wraps.
29th row: P16, wrap 1, turn.
30th and 31st rows: K17,
wrap 1, turn. P18, wrap 1, turn.
Work 16 rows more as set, working 1 st more before the wrap on every row, ending with p34, wrap 1, turn.
48th and 49th rows: K35,
wrap 1, turn. P36, wrap 1, turn. *
50th row: K to end. ***
Break off Lime and using Navy, p 1 row.

REST OF FOOT

Beginning with a k row and starting stripe sequence after 4th Navy row, ss 58 rows, finishing with 6 Red rows and 2 Lime rows. Break off Red and continue in Lime only.

DIVIDE FOR TOE

K39 and slip these sts onto a st holder. Working on remaining 40 sts, work 2nd to 49th rows as given for heel from * to *.
50th row: K to last 3 sts,
k2tog, k1 – 39 sts.
Hold these remaining 39 sts with the sts from toe st holder with right sides together and taking 1 st from each side and working them together, cast off toe sts.

To make up

Join the side seam using a mattress stitch.

Contrast Heel Socks (both alike)

With 2.75mm needles and Lime yarn, cast on 79 sts.
Work rib as given for the
Striped Socks to **.
Break off Lime and join in Navy.
Beginning with a k row, ss
77 rows, ending with wrong side facing.
Join in Lime at this edge, leaving Navy still attached.
Divide for heel: Work as given for Striped Socks from
*** to ***.
Break off Lime and using Navy, p 1 row.

REST OF FOOT

Ss 58 rows.
Break off Navy and continue in Lime only.
Complete as given for
Striped Socks from ****.

Plain-ish Socks (both alike)

With 2.75mm needles and
Red yarn, cast on 79 sts.
Work rib as given for the Striped Socks to **.
Join in Lime. Beginning
with a k row, ss 2 rows.
Break off Lime.
With Red, ss 75 rows, ending with wrong side facing.

DIVIDE FOR HEEL

Work as given for Striped Socks from *** to ***.

REST OF FOOT

Beginning with a p row, ss 57 rows. Join in Lime and ss another 2 rows. Break off Lime and continue in Red only. Complete as given for Striped Socks from ****.

Contrast Heel Socks

Moss stitch neck warmer

This cosy neck warmer is quick to make in a simple moss stitch pattern that will keep you warm as well as looking fab

What you need

4 x 50g (50m) skeins Mirasol Sulka in:
- Rosewood
- 6mm circular needle, 60cm long
- Stitch marker
- Yarn needle

FINISHED MEASUREMENTS
Circumference : 68cm (27in).
Depth : 27cm (10½in).

TENSION
13 sts and 24 rows in pattern in the round to measure 10x10cm (4x4in) using 6mm (US 10) needles.

ABBREVIATIONS
K, knit; **st(s)**, stitches; **p**, purl

Using 6mm circular needles, cast on 91sts.

Join stitches to work in the round as follows: Spread stitches out along the cable/wire and bring the tips of the needles together.

Make sure that your stitches are not twisted.

Move the top stitch from the right hand needle to the left hand needle, then k2tog. This will close the gap between the first and last stitch. Place a stitch marker at this spot, which will mark the beginning of each round. (90 sts).

Round 1 (RS): *K1, P1; rep from * to the end.

Round 2: *P1, K1; rep from * to the end.

Repeat Rounds 1-2, until work measures 27cm deep, ending at the stitch marker.

Cast off.

To make up

Sew in all remaining ends on wrong side. Although it is not essential to block, the appearance of your cowl will be enhanced if you do so.
You can gently block by pinning out flat to dimensions given. Spray liberally with cool water to moisten, patting the water into the knitting until thoroughly dampened. Leave to try dry completely before unpinning.

Pattern by
Sian Brown

After doing a Fashion/Textiles BA Sian worked supplying to high street retailers on machine knits. She became interested in handknits and have designed these since, working for magazines, publishers and yarn companies.
www.sianbrown.co.uk

Clothing | 59

Quick & Easy KNITTING

What you need

1 x 100g (224m) West Yorkshire Spinners Bluefaced Leicester DK Prints in:

- Bluetit

Or another equivalent Chunky weight yarn

- 3.5mm (US 4) needles
- 4mm (US 6) needles
- Stitch holders
- Stitch markers
- Yarn needle

TENSION

22 stitches and 28 rows = 10cm (4in) in stocking stitch using 4mm needles.

ABBREVIATIONS

St(s), stitches; k, knit; p, purl; tog, together; m, make one

Pattern by
Lynne Rowe

Lynne Rowe is a knit and crochet designer, technical editor, craft author and tutor. She loves to pass on her skills to help others to knit, crochet and create.
www.thewoolnest.blogspot.co.uk. & www.knitcrochetcreate.com

Cosy mittens

Clothing

Use two straight needles to knit up a pair of simple mittens that will become an essential part of your winter wardrobe

Size		S	M/L
To fit adult hand	cm in	19.5 21½	21.5 8½

RIB

Using 3.5mm needles, cast on 45 [49] sts.
Row 1: (K1, P1) to the last st, K1
Row 2: (P1, K1) to the last st, P1.
Repeat Rows 1-2 until rib measures approximately 8 [9] cm from the start. Change to 4mm needles and continue with thumb gusset.

THUMB GUSSET

Row 1 (dec): K2tog, K to end. 44 [48] sts.
Row 2: Purl. 44 [48] sts.
Row 3 (inc): K21 [23], m1, K2, m1, K21 [23]. (46 [50] sts)
Rows 4-6: Beg with P row, st st 3 rows.
Row 7 (inc): K21 [23], m1, K4, m1, K21 [23]. (48 [52] sts)
Rows 8-10: Beg with P row, st st 3 rows.
Row 11 (inc): K21 [23], m1, K6, m1, K21 [23]. (50 [54] sts)
Rows 12-14: Beg with P row, st st 3 rows.
Row 15 (inc): K21 [23], m1, K8, m1, K21 [23]. (52 [56] sts)
Rows 16-18: Beg with p row, st st 3 rows.
Row 19 (inc): K21 [23], m1, K10, m1, K21 [23]. (54 [58] sts)
Rows 20-22: Beg with P row, st st 3 rows.

FOR L ONLY:

Row 23 (inc): K23, m1, K12, m1, K23. (60 sts)
Rows 24-26: Beg with P row, st st 3 rows.

THUMB

Row 1: K33 [37], slip remaining 21 [23] sts to stitch holder 1, turn.
Row 2: Cast on 2 sts, then P12 [14]. S rem 21 [23] sts to stitch holder 2, turn.
Row 3: Cast on 2 sts then K16 [18]. Beginning with a P row, work in st st until thumb measures 5 [5.75] cm (or length required).

Next Row (dec): (k2tog) to the end. (8 [9] sts)
Cut yarn leaving a long tail and thread through rem sts. Pull tight to fasten and secure gathers with a couple of stitches. Use the tail end to stitch the thumb seam, down to the cast on sts.
With right side facing, slip the stitches from stitch holder 2 onto the right hand needle (these are the stitches to the right of the thumb - don't knit these as they've already been knitted). Re-join yarn - note: you will notice that the yarn is self-striping and that there is a colour sequence that is noticeable on your mittens. Due to knitting the thumb, the self-striping pattern will now be out of sequence, so you will need to wind off (and cut out) a length of yarn until you reach the correct part of the yarn to continue with the main striping sequence. Pick up and knit 4 sts from the base of the thumb, then K across sts from stitch holder 1. 46 [50] sts.
Next Row (dec): P21 [23], (p2tog) twice, P21 [23]. 44 [48] sts.
Continue with Hand section.

HAND

Beginning with a K row, work in st st until hand measures 9 [11.5] cm from the base of thumb.

FOR SMALL SIZE ONLY:

Next Row (dec): (K20, k2tog) twice. 42 sts.
Next Row: Purl. 42 sts.

FOR ALL SIZES:

Next Row (dec): (K4, k2tog) to end. 35 [40] sts.
Beg with a P row, st st 3 rows.
Next Row (dec): (K3, k2tog) to end. 28 [32] sts.
Beg with a P row, st st 3 rows.
Next Row (dec): (K2, k2tog) to end. 21 [24] sts.
Next Row: Purl. 21 [24] sts.
Next Row (dec): (K1, k2tog) to end. 14 [16] sts.
Next Row (dec): (p2tog) to end. 7 [8] sts.

To make up

Cut yarn leaving a long tail to stitch the seam and thread through rem sts. Pull tight to fasten and secure gathers with a few stitches. Tie off and trim all loose yarn ends inside the glove (except for the long tail end). Use the tail end to stitch the side seam and rib seam.

Quick & Easy KNITTING

Eylet twigs top

What you need

1 x 500g (110m) Sirdar Amalfi DK
75% cotton, 25% viscose in:

- Atrani
Or a similar DK weight yarn
- Pair each of 3.25 mm (US 3)
  knitting needles
- 4mm (US 6) knitting needles
- Stitch holders
- Yarn needle

TENSION

22 sts x 28 rows = 10cm (4in)
over stocking stitch using size 4mm
needles.

ABBREVIATIONS

St(s), stitch(es); k, knit; yo, yarn over;
psso, pass slip st over; p, purl; sl,
slip; tog, together; p2togb, p2tog
through back of sts; inc, increase (k
into front then back of same st);
dec, decrease (by taking 2 sts tog);
ss, stocking st (k on right side and p
on wrong side); skpo, (sl1, k1, pass sl
st over); nil, nothing; mb, make
bobble

Clothing

Add to your winter wardrobe with this wonderful lace-wielding top, perfect for those cosy nights in

Size		XS	S	S/M	M	M/L	L	XL	XXL
To fit bust	cm	82	86	92	97	102	107	112	117
Finished bust	cm	87	92	98	103	109	114	120	125
Length to shoulder	cm	53	54	55	56	57	58	59	60
Sleeve length	cm	30	30	30	30	30	30	30	30

PATT PANEL
(WORKED OVER 16 STS)

Row 1: K2, yo, k3tog, yo, K3, yo, sl 1, k2tog, psso, yo, K5.
Row 2 and every foll wrong side row: Purl.
Row 3: K1, yo, k3tog, yo, K5, yo, sl 1, k2tog, psso, yo, K4.
Row 5: Mb, K5, yo, k3tog, yo, K1, yo, sl 1, k2tog, psso, yo, K3.
Row 7: K5, yo, k3tog, yo, K3, yo, sl 1, k2tog, psso, yo, K2.
Row 9: K4, yo, k3tog, yo, K5, yo, sl 1, k2tog, psso, yo, Mb.
Row 11: K3, yo, k3tog, yo, K1, yo, sl 1, k2tog, psso, yo, K6.
Row 12: Purl.
These 12 rows form the patt.

BACK
With 3.25mm needles cast on 98 [104 : 110 : 116 : 122 : 128 : 134 : 140] sts.
K 5 rows.
Change to 4mm needles.
Work in patt.
Row 1: K41 [44 : 47 : 50 : 53 : 56 : 59 : 62] , work next 16 sts as Row 1 of patt panel, K41 [44 : 47 : 50 : 53 : 56 : 59 : 62] .
Row 2: Purl.
Row 3: K41 [44 : 47 : 50 : 53 : 56 : 59 :62] , work next 16 sts as Row 3 of patt panel, K41 [44 : 47 : 50 : 53 : 56 : 59 : 62]
Row 4: Purl.
These 4 rows set st st with central patt panel.
Work a further 4 rows.
Next Row (dec): K7, skpo, K to last 9 sts, k2tog, K7.
Work 11 rows.
Rep the last 12 rows once more and the dec row again. (92 [98 : 104 : 110 : 116 : 122 : 128 : 134] sts)
Work 15 [15 : 17 : 17 : 19 : 19 : 21 : 21] rows.
Next Row (inc): K7, m1, K to last 7 sts, m1, K7.
Work 11 rows.
Rep the last 12 rows once more and the inc row again. (98 [104 : 110 : 116 : 122 : 128 : 134 : 140] sts)
Cont straight until Back measures 32 [33 : 33 : 34 : 34 : 35 : 35 : 36] cm (12 ½ [13 : 13 : 13 ½ : 13 ½ : 13 ¾ : 13 ¾ : 14 ¼] in) from cast on edge, ending with a P row.

SHAPE RAGLAN ARMHOLES
Cast off 4 [5 : 6 : 7 : 8 : 9 : 10 : 11] sts at beg of next 2 rows. (90 [94 : 98 : 102 : 106 : 110 : 114 : 118] sts)
Next Row (dec): K2, skpo, K to last 4 sts, k2tog, K2.
Next Row: Purl. **
Rep the last 2 rows 23 [24 : 25 : 26 : 27 : 28 : 29 : 30] times and the first row once more. (40 [42 : 44 : 46 : 48 : 50 : 52 : 54] sts)
Next Row (dec): P2tog, p to last 2 sts, p2tog.
Leave these 38 [40 : 42 : 44 : 46 : 48 : 50 : 52] sts on a stitch holder.

FRONT
Work as given for Back to **.
Rep the last 2 rows 8 [9 : 10 : 11 : 12 : 13 : 14 : 15] times more. (72 [74 : 76 : 78 : 80 : 82 : 84 : 86] sts)

SHAPE FRONT NECK
Next Row (dec): K2, skpo, K20, turn and work on these 23 sts.
Next Row: Purl.
Next Row (dec): K2, skpo, K to last 4 sts, k2tog, K2.
Next Row: Purl.
Next Row (dec): K2, skpo, K to end.
Next Row: Purl.
Rep these 4 rows 4 times. 8 sts
Next Row (dec): K2, skpo, K to end.
Next Row: Purl.
Rep these 2 rows 4 times. 3 sts
Cast off.
With RS facing place centre 24 [26 : 28 : 30 : 32 : 34 : 36 : 38] sts on a stitch holder, rejoin yarn to rem sts, K to last 4 sts, k2tog, K2. (23 sts)
Next Row: Purl.
Next Row (dec): K2, skpo, K to last 4 sts, k2tog, K2.
Next Row: Purl.
Next Row (dec): K to last 4 sts, k2tog, K2.

Next Row: Purl.
Rep these 4 rows 4 times. (8 sts)
Next Row (dec): K to last 4 sts, k2tog, K2.
Next Row: Purl.
Rep these 2 rows 4 times. (3 sts)
Cast off.

SLEEVES

With 3.25mm needles cast on 50 [54 : 58 : 62 : 66 : 70 : 74 : 78] sts.
K 3 rows.
Change to 4mm needles.
Work in patt.
Row 1: K17 [19 : 21 : 23 : 25 : 27 : 29 : 31], work next 16 sts as Row 1 of patt panel, K17 [19 : 21 : 23 : 25 : 27 : 29 :31].
Row 2: Purl.
Row 3: K17 [19 : 21 : 23 : 25 : 27 : 29 : 31], work next 16 sts as Row 3 of patt panel, K17 [19 : 21 : 23 : 25 : 27 : 29 : 31]
Row 4: Purl.
These 4 rows set the patt panel.
Work a further 4 rows.
Next Row (inc): K3, m1, K to last 3 sts, m1, K3.
Work 7 rows.
Rep the last 8 rows 6 times and the inc row again. (66 [70 : 74 : 78 : 82 : 86 : 90 : 94] sts)

Cont straight until Sleeve measures 30cm (12in) from cast on edge, ending with a WS row.

SHAPE SLEEVE TOP

Cast off 4 [5 : 6 : 7 : 8 : 9 : 10 : 11] sts at beg of next 2 rows. 58 [60 : 62 : 64 : 66 : 68 : 70 : 72] sts
Next Row (dec): K2, skpo, K to last 4 sts, k2tog, K2.
Next Row: Purl.
Next Row: Knit.
Next Row: Purl.
Rep the last 4 rows 5 times more. 46 [48 : 50 : 52 : 54 : 56 : 58 : 60] sts
Next Row (dec): K2, skpo, K to last 4 sts, k2tog, K2.
Next Row: Purl.
Rep the last 2 rows 11 [12 : 13 : 14 : 15 : 16 : 17 : 18] times and the first row again. (20 sts)
Next Row (dec): P2tog, p to last 2 sts, p2tog.
Leave these 18 sts on a stitch holder.

NECKBAND

Join both front and right back raglan seams.
With right side facing, using 3.25mm needles, K18 sts from left sleeve, pick up and K22 sts down left side of front neck, K24 [26 : 28 : 30 : 32 : 34 : 36 : 38] sts from left front holder, pick up and K22 sts up right side of front neck, K18 sts from right sleeve, 38 [40 : 42 : 44 : 46 : 48 : 50 : 52] sts from back neck holder.
K 4 rows.
Cast off.

To make up

Join left back raglan seam and neckband. Join side and sleeve seams.

Quick & Easy KNITTING

Stormy waters shawl

A lightweight, dynamic and modern shawl, this item makes a great and fast project

What you need

1 x 100g (500m) Angora Gold Simli (10% mohair, 10% wool, 5% metallic, 75% acrylic) in:
- Peacock
- 4ply (fingering) weight yarn in your chosen colour
- 5.5mm needles. If using different weight yarn, use needles at least three sizes up from stated on the label to keep fabric airy and light
- A piece of cardboard for tassels
- Blocking mats and pins
- Yarn needle

FINISHED SIZE

180cm (71in) long, excluding tassels. 80cm (31in) at the widest part.

TENSION

Work 18 sts and 28 rows in garter stitch when blocked, to measure 10x10cm/4x4in using 5.5mm (US 9) needles, or size required to obtain correct tension.

Tension is not critical and can be changed to fit the desired yarn.

ABBREVIATIONS

St(s), stitch(es); **k**, knit; **p**, purl; **yo**, yarn over; **gst**, garter stitch (every row k); **wyif**, with yarn in front; **kfb**, knit front and back; **sl**, slip

SET UP ROWS

Using 5.5mm needles, cast on 3 sts.
Row 1 (WS): K3. (3 sts).
Row 2 (RS): sl 1 wyif, K2.
Row 3: Sl 1 wyif, K2.
Row 4: Sl 1 wyif, Kfb, K1. (4 sts).
Row 5: Sl 1 wyif, K3.
Row 6: Sl 1 wyif, knit until last 2 sts, Kfb, K1. (5 sts).
Row 7: Sl 1 wyif, knit until the end of the row.
Row 8: As Row 6. (6 sts).
Row 9: As Row 7.
Row 10: As Row 6. (7 sts).

BODY OF SHAWL

The shawl is knitted by implementing a 4-stripe pattern sequence in the following order.
16 rows: Garter Stripe 1
8 rows: Net Stripe
16 rows: Garter Stripe 2
12 rows: Lace Stripe
NOTE: See stripe patterns below for the instructions for each section.
The number of repetitions may vary depending on the yarn, gauge and desired size of the shawl.

Row count follows. In the row count, the usual text corresponds to the sample shawl.

The text in italics is added for your convenience and can be used for additional rows.

Regardless of the yarn choice or gauge, the last stripe of the shawl has to be a Garter Stripe. This will help to keep the shape of the finished garment.

Stripe patterns

GARTER STRIPE 1

(16 rows, increase by 8 sts overall)
Row 1 (WS): Sl 1 wyif, knit until the end of the row.
Row 2 (RS): Sl 1 wyif, knit until last 2 sts, Kfb, K1.
Rows 3–16: Repeat Rows 1-2 another 7 times.

NET STRIPE

(8 rows, increase by 4 sts overall)
Row 1 (WS): Sl 1 wyif, (yo, K2tog) until the end of the row.
Row 2 (RS): Sl 1 wyif, (yo, K2tog) until last 2 sts, yo, Kfb, K1.
Row 3: Sl 1 wyif, K1, (yo, K2tog) until the end of the row.

NOTE

The shawl is knitted from the right corner with increases at the end of every RS row. Increases are made in the form of kfb unless stated otherwise. The neat braid-like edge of the shawl is created by slipping first stitches. In every row first st is slipped as if to purl with yarn in the front (abbreviation is sl 1 wyif), and every last st is knitted.

Row count is included in the pattern.

The number of completed rows can be changed depending on the yarn/gauge/desired size of a shawl. The usual text corresponds to the sample shawl. The text in italics is added for your convenience and can be used for additional rows.

If you'd like to make tassels, save yarn for them in advance: 2 tassels require approximately 26ft (8m).

Quick & Easy KNITTING

Tip
This pattern can be used as a base for experiments, as neither yarn weight nor tension is critical.

Row 4: Sl 1 wyif, (yo, K2tog) until last st, yo, K1.

Rows 5-8: Repeat Rows 1-4 once more.

GARTER STRIPE 2
(16 rows, increase by 8 sts overall)
Row 1 (WS): Sl 1 wyif, purl until last st, K1.
Row 2 (RS): Sl 1 wyif, knit until last 2 sts, Kfb, K1.
Row 3: Sl 1 wyif, knit until the end of the row.
Row 4: Sl 1 wyif, knit until last 2 sts, Kfb, K1.
Rows 5-16: Repeat Rows 3-4 another 6 times.

LACE STRIPE
(12 rows, increase by 6 sts overall)
Row 1 (WS): Sl 1 wyif, knit until the end of the row.
Row 2 (RS): Sl 1 wyif, (K1, yo) until last 2 sts, Kfb, K1.
Row 3: Sl 1 wyif, purl until last stitch, K1.
Row 4: Sl 1 wyif, k1, (k2tog) until last 2 sts, Kfb, K1.
Row 5: Sl 1 wyif, purl until last stitch, K1.
Row 6: Sl 1 wyif, (yo, k2tog) until last 2 sts, yo, k2.
Row 7: Sl 1 wyif, knit until the end of the row.
Row 8: Sl 1 wyif, (yo, k1) until last stitch, K1.
Row 9: Sl 1 wyif, purl until last stitch, K1.
Row 10: Sl 1 wyif, (k2tog) until last 3 sts, K1, Kfb, K1.
Row 11: Sl 1 wyif, purl until last stitch, K1.
Row 12: Sl 1 wyif, (yo, k2tog) until last 3 sts, K1, Kfb, K1.

ROW COUNTS
Rows 11-26: Garter Stripe 1. (15 sts).
Rows 27-34: Net Stripe. (19 sts).
Rows 35-50: Garter Stripe 2. (27 sts).
Rows 51-62: Lace Stripe. (33 sts).
Rows 63-78: Garter Stripe 1. (15 sts).
Rows 79-86: Net Stripe. (19 sts).
Rows 87-102: Garter Stripe 2. (27 sts).
Rows 103-114: Lace Stripe. (33 sts).
Rows 115-130: Garter Stripe 1. (41 sts).
Rows 131-138: Net Stripe. (45 sts).
Rows 139-154: Garter Stripe 2. (53 sts).
Rows 155-166: Lace Stripe. (59 sts).
Rows 167-182: Garter Stripe 1 (67 sts).
Rows 183-190: Net Stripe. (71 sts).
Rows 191-206: Garter Stripe 2. (79 sts).
Rows 207-218: Lace Stripe. (85 sts).
Rows 219-234: Garter Stripe 1. (93 sts).
Rows 235-242: Net Stripe. (97 sts).
Rows 243-258: Garter Stripe 2. (105 sts).
Rows 259-270: Lace Stripe. (111 sts).
Rows 271-286: Garter Stripe 1. (119 sts).
Rows 287-294: Net Stripe. (123 sts).
Rows 295-310: Garter Stripe 2. (131 sts).
Rows 311-322: Lace Stripe. (137 sts).
Rows 323-338: Garter Stripe 1. (145 sts).
Rows 339-346: Net Stripe. (149 sts).
Rows 347-362: Garter Stripe 2. (157 sts).
Rows 363-374: Lace Stripe. (163 sts).
Rows 375-390: Garter Stripe 1. (171 sts).
Rows 391-398: Net Stripe.

Clothing 69

Pattern by
Ksenia Naidyon
Ksenia designs cozy knitwear and home decor that are a pleasure both to knit and to use. Her patterns feature modern color palettes, interesting textures, and comfortable fit.
lifeiscozy.com

(175 sts).
Rows 399-414: Garter Stripe 2. (183 sts).
Rows 415-426: Lace Stripe. (189 sts).
Rows 427-442: Garter Stripe 1. (197 sts).
Rows 443-450: Net Stripe. (201 sts).
Rows 451-466: Garter Stripe 2. (209 sts).
Rows 467-478: Lace Stripe. (215 sts).
Rows 479-494: Garter Stripe 1. (223 sts).
Rows 495-502: Net Stripe. (227 sts).
Rows 503-518: Garter Stripe 2 (235 sts).
Rows 519-530: Lace Stripe. (241 sts).

To make up

Regardless of the yarn choice or gauge, the last stripe of the shawl has to be a Garter Stripe. This will help keep the shape of the finished garment.

This shawl was finished after completing row 337. You can stop after completing any WS row of a Garter Stripe, depending on when the skein comes to the end.

Bind off very loosely as follows: K1, (slip stitch back to left needle, K2tog) until 1 stitch is left.

Cut yarn leaving a tail of approx 20cm (8in) and pull it through the loop of the last stitch.

Wash the shawl in 30ºC water and block into shape. Moderate stretching is recommended to open up the yarn overs and garter stitch.

Make 2 tassels approx. 7.5cm (3in) long and secure them with the ends of working yarn at the beginning and end of the shawl. Hide the ends of yarn in the tassels.

Fairy tale legwarmers

These legwarmers make ideal companions for woodland walks and warm evenings curled up with a book and hot chocolate

What you need

1 x 200m (218yds) per 100g ball of Rowan Pure Wool Worsted, 100% superwash wool in:
- Colour 1: Dark red
- Colour 2: Cream
yarn in your chosen colour
Or another equivalent weight yarn
- 4 mm (US 6) set of 5 DPNs (or circular needle and magic loop technique if preferred)
- Stitch markers
- Yarn needle
- Pompom maker (optional)

FINISHED SIZE
18cm (7in) wide x 13cm (5in) deep.

TENSION
One size to fit calf up to 15in with negative ease. Circumference around leg measures 28cm (11in). Circumference around ankle measures 20cm (8in), 28cm (11in) long, laid flat.

ABBREVIATIONS
St(s), stitch(es); **k**, knit; **p**, purl; **k2tog**, knit two together

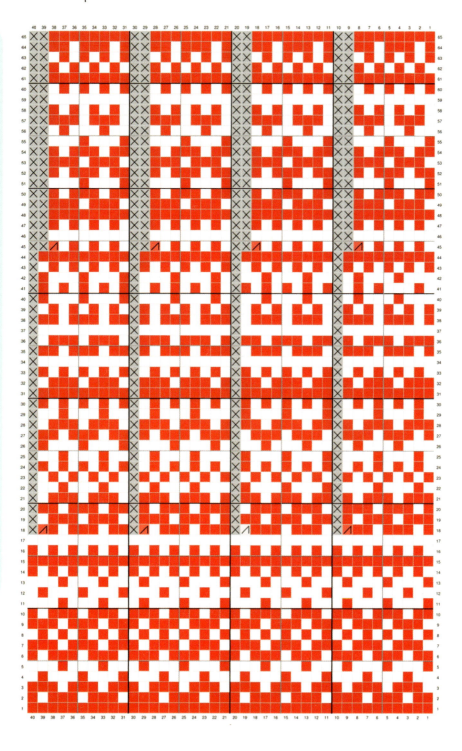

Legwarmers (make 2)

With col 1, cast on 80 sts loosely. Taking care not to twist cast on edge, arrange sts evenly over 4 DPNs, place maker and work in rounds.

TOP CUFF

Rnd 1: *K1, P1; rep from * to end.
Rnd 1 forms 1x1 rib. Work a further 11 rnds in 1x1 rib (work a few more rnds if you prefer a deeper cuff).

FAIR ISLE

Rnds 1-17: K40 sts of the chart (left) twice.
Rnd 18 (dec): (K8 as per chart, k2tog) 8 times. 72 sts
Rnds 19-44: K36 sts of chart twice.
Rnd 45 (dec): (K7 as per chart, k2tog) 8 times. 64 sts
Rnds 46-65: K32 sts of chart twice.

BOTTOM CUFF

Work in 1x1 rib for 12 rnds.
Work a few more rnds if you prefer a deeper cuff.
Cast off loosely in rib.

To make up

Weave in ends. Wash the legwarmers gently in lukewarm water and block them.

Optional pompoms

Make 2 pompoms approx 3.5cm (1¼in) in diameter. Take 3 lengths of yarn approx 50cm (20in) long and twist to make a braid. Secure a pompom to each end of the braid, then sew the middle of the braid to the upper part of a legwarmer (at the border of the ribbing and the fair isle). Make a bow and pull it tight. Secure the bow with another stitch or two at its middle.
Repeat for the second legwarmer.

Clothing 71

Pattern by
Ksenia Naidyon
Ksenia designs cozy knitwear and home decor that are a pleasure both to knit and to use. Her patterns feature modern color palettes, interesting textures, and comfortable fit.
lifeiscozy.com

Tip
To ensure cuffs are not too tight, use the larger needle to cast on and cast off (remembering to switch to the smaller needle as soon as you have cast on).

Simple lace scarf

Combine the increase and decrease techniques to create a feminine and pretty lace scarf

What you need

402m (440yds) 3-ply Malabrigo Sock 100% wool yarn in:
- Aguas
- 4mm (US 6) needles
- 2 removable stitch markers
- Tapestry needle

FINISHED SIZE
Approximately 22x160cm (9x63in).

TENSION
25 sts and 26 rows = 10cm (4in) in Lace Pattern 2.

ABBREVIATIONS
St(s), stitch(es); **k**, knit; **p**, purl; **sl**, slip; **tog**, together; **p2togb**, p2tog through back of sts; **inc**, increase (k into front then back of same st); **dec**, decrease (by taking 2 sts tog); **ss**, stocking st (k on right side and p on wrong side); **skpo**, (sl1, k1, pass sl st over); **nil**, meaning nothing is worked here for this size; **sm**, slip marker

NOTE

If you find charts difficult to work with, don't despair. Many designers usually provide written versions of stitch patterns for those knitters who prefer to use them. If not, it is very easy to create your own. All you need to do is write down the stitches in each row, remembering to read right side (RS) rows from right to left and wrong side (WS) rows from left to right.

Simple lace scarf

Cast (bind) on 55 sts.
Knit 4 rows.

Next row: K3, PM, following the chart or written instructions, work Lace Pattern 1, working the sts enclosed by the red lines 6 times in total, PM, K3.

NOTE: The markers are there to remind you that the three stitches at either edge are to be worked in garter stitch as a border. Garter stitch is great for borders on scarves and shawls as it prevents the edges of the work from curling in.
You might want to add more markers in different colours from the edging markers between each repeat of the lace pattern across your scarf to help you keep track of where you are in the pattern. To do this, add a marker to your needle between every set of 8 stitches (not including the edging stitches).

Continue following the chart or written directions for Lace Pattern 1, using the key to identify the different stitches used, until you have completed all 16 rows shown.
   Then repeat those 16 rows a further 2 times.
   Knit 4 rows.

Next row: K3, sm, following the chart or written instructions, work Lace Pattern 2, working the sts enclosed by the red lines 6 times in total, sm, K3.

NOTE: If you used extra stitch markers to divide up your repeats of the lace pattern, you need to remove these and reposition them as Lace Pattern 2 has a different number of stitches in each repeat than Lace Pattern 1. Lace Pattern 2 has 6 stitches in a repeat, so you need to place a stitch marker between each set of 6 stitches (not including the edging stitches). Note that on the chart there is a single stitch after the border sts, but before the first pattern repeat, so you might want to place a stitch marker after that stitch to remind you where your first pattern repeat begins.

Continue following the chart or written directions for Lace Pattern 2 until you have completed all 12 rows of the chart. Then repeat those 12 rows a further 21 times.
   Knit 4 rows.
Next row: K3, sm, following chart or written instructions, work Lace Pattern 3, working the sts enclosed by the red lines 8 times in total, sm, K3.

NOTE: If you are using the optional stitch markers, you need to move them to 8-stitch intervals as for the first chart.

Continue following the chart or written directions for Lace Pattern 3 until you have completed all 16 rows of the chart. Then repeat those 16 rows a further 2 times.
   Knit 4 rows.
   Cast (bind) off.

To make up

Lace always needs to be blocked to bring out its best qualities. Simply soak the scarf in water with a little wool wash added, rinse it, and squeeze out as much water as possible.
   Wrapping it in a towel and then treading all over it is a pretty good way to get the most water out of it once you have squeezed out as much as you can by hand. Don't wring your knitting, just squeeze it firmly. You don't want to felt it!
   Once you have removed as much water as possible, pin out the scarf to the dimensions given in the pattern on a soft surface such as blocking mats. If you don't have blocking mats, a carpet or a spare bed works just as well.
   As you pin out the scarf, you will see that the lace opens out so that you can see the pattern created by all those decreases and yarn overs.
   Try to keep the edges of the scarf straight either by using blocking wires threaded through or lots of pins short distances apart so as not to make scalloped edges down the sides.
   Leave the scarf pinned out until it is completely dry, then unpin, sew in any ends and wear with pride!

Picot-topped ankle socks

Learn how to make this pretty project using the below pattern and achieve a decoratively topped sock you can be proud of

What you need

250m (275yd) 4 ply yarn Rowan Fine Art yarn in:
- Rowan
- 2.75mm (US 2) 5x double-pointed needles (DPNs)
- 1 stitch marker
- Tapestry needle

FINISHED SIZE
UK size 6 (US size 8), length can be adjusted – see notes in the pattern.

TENSION
30 stitches and 38 rounds = 10cm (4in) in stocking (stockinette) stitch (st st).

ABBREVIATIONS
St(s), stitch(es); **k**, knit; **p**, purl; **sl**, slip; **k2tog**, k 2 sts together (to decrease 1 st); **ssk**, slip slip knit; **yo**, yarn over; **patt**, pattern

NOTE
Alternatively, to work a shorter or longer foot, measure the wearer's foot from the back of the heel to the base of the big toe. Use this measurement in place of the measurement above.

Picot-topped ankle socks

Cast (bind) 60 sts.
Arrange over 4 needles as follows:
Needles 1 & 3: 16 sts.
Needles 2 & 4: 14 sts, being careful not to twist the stitches.
Slip the first stitch on the LH needle onto the RH needle, then pass the first stitch on the RH needle over the top of the stitch you just slipped and place it on the LH needle. This will be the first stitch you work.
Place a stitch marker between stitches 1 and 2 to denote the beginning of the round.
Rnd 1: (K1, P1) to end of rnd.
Rep Rnd 1 3 more times.
Next rnd: (K2tog, yo) to end of rnd. This will create the pretty picot edge around the top of the sock.
Rep round 1 4 more times.
Knit 8 rounds.
Next rnd: (K2, k2tog, yo) to end of rnd.
Knit 4 rounds.
Next rnd: (k2tog, yo, K2) to end of rnd.
Knit 8 rounds
NOTE: For a longer sock cuff, add more knit rounds here.

DIVIDE FOR HEEL

Knit the first 30 sts on to one needle, leaving the rem sts on 2 spare needles.
Turn and working in rows on the first 30 sts, work as follows:
Row 1: Sl1, P to end.
Row 2: Sl1, K to end.
Repeat these 2 rows 8 times more. Then work Row 1 again.

TURN HEEL

Row 1 (RS): Sl1, K16, ssk, K1. Turn work.
Row 2 (WS): Sl1, P5, p2tog, P1. Turn work.
Row 3 (RS): Sl1, K6, ssk, K1. Turn work.
Row 4 (WS): Sl1, P7, p2tog, P1. Turn work.

Cont in this way, working 1 more st each row before dec until 18 sts remain.
Next row: Sl1, K to last 2 sts, ssk.
Next row: Sl 1, P to last 2 sts, p2tog. (16 sts)

GUSSET

With RS facing, K8 sts onto one needle.
Needle 1 (next needle): K next 8 sts, then pick up and K 10 sts down side of heel.
Needle 2: Knit across 30 sts that were held on spare needles.
Needle 3: Pick up and K10 sts up side of heel flap, then K the 8 sts on the first needle.
Continue as follows:
Rnd 1:
Needle 1 (dec): K to last 3 sts, k2tog, K1.
Needle 2: K all sts.
Needle 3 (dec): K1, ssk, K to end of needle.
Rnd 2: Knit all sts.
Rep last 2 rnds until:
Needle 1: 15 sts rem.
Needle 2: 30 sts.
Needle 3: 15 sts rem.
Now knit every round until work, from heel to needles, measures 20cm (8in).

SHAPE TOE

Rnd 1:
Needle 1 (dec): K to last 3 sts, k2tog, K1.
Needle 2 (dec): K1, ssk, K to last 3 sts, k2tog, K1.
Needle 3 (dec): K1, ssk, K to end of needle.
Rnd 2: Knit all sts.
Rep last 2 rounds until 40 sts rem.
Rep round 1 until 24 sts rem.
Place stitches from needles 1 and 3 onto one needle. With RS facing, graft the toe using kitchener stitch.

To make up

Darn in ends. Turn sock inside out, and fold the cuff over so that the cast (bind)-on edge is in line with the last row of rib stitching. You will now see that the picot edge is visible. With needle and yarn, join the cast (bind)-off edge to the body of the sock, along the line of the last rib round.

Quick & Easy KNITTING

Fair Isle boot cuffs

Add flair to your plain boots with these Fair Isle boot cuffs.

What you need

1 x of DK yarn each in:
- Colour 1: Dove
- Colour 2: Raspberry
- Colour 3: Primrose
- Colour 4: Spring Green
- Colour 5: Lilac
- Colour 6: Thistle
- Colour 7: Leaf
- 4mm (US 6) double-pointed needles
- 2 removable stitch markers
- Tapestry needle

FINISHED SIZE

Size S/M fits calves up to 34cm (13.5in).
L fits up too about 40cm (15.75in).
Total length: 13cm (5in).
Width (when laid flat): For S/M: 15cm (6in) and for L 19cm (7.5in).
As with most knitted accessories the boot cuffs are very stretchy.

TENSION

24 sts over 30 rows = 10cm (4in) in Fair Isle pattern using needle 4mm (US 6).

ABBREVIATIONS

St(s), stitch(es); **k**, knit; **p**, purl; **k2tog**, knit two together

Fair Isle boot cuffs

With col 1 and double-pointed needles (DPNs) cast (bind) on 72 (88) sts (18 sts on each needle for S/M, 22 sts on each for L). Join to work in the round and don't twist the cast (bind)-on edge as you do so.

Rnd 1: *K2, P2, rep from * to end.
Next rnd: Work in rib K2, P2.
Continue in K2, p2rib for a further 7 rnds.
Work the chart.

Continuing with col 1 and in K2 P2 rib as set previously, work 16 rnds.
Cast (bind) off loosely in rib.

To make up

Make the other boot cuff the same way. Weave in loose ends and block carefully by using an iron set on wool with the steam function on. Wear proudly!

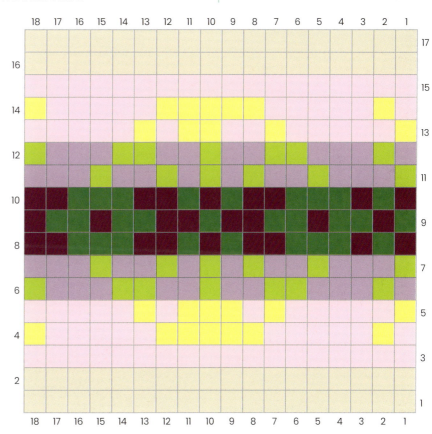

NOTE

There are seven colours at work in the project and that can seem overwhelming. You never use more than two in the same round, so concentrate on that. Cut the main colour yarn when you have finished the upper rib and the first two rounds of the chart. Then you have one less thread.

Home

PATTERNS

82
Graduating stripes place mat

84
Trio of dishcloths

86
Placemat & coasters

87
I-cord coasters

88
Simple cushion

89
Gadget cosies

90
Textured draught excluder

92
Basket stitch container

94
Blackberry stitch tea cosy

96
Bobbles tea cosy

98
Chevron cushion cover

100
Willowherb lace doily

102
Simple baby blankets

104
Strawberry pie blanket

Graduating stripes place mat

Brighten up your dining table with these super simple table settings

What you need

FOR THE SET

For this pattern you shall require 1x Ball of an Aran Weight yarn:
- Teal
- Light Grey
- White
- 4mm (US 6) knitting needles
- 2 x 1.4mm buttons
- Sewing needle and thread

FINISHED SIZE

Length (approx): 23.5cm (9.25in).
Width (approx): 31.5cm (12.5in).

TENSION

18 sts and 32 rows = 10cm (4in) in moss (seed) stitch on 4mm (US 6) needles.

ABBREVIATIONS

K, knit; **p**, purl; **st(s)**, stitch(es)

PATTERN REQUIRES:

Moss (seed) stitch
*K1, P1; rep from * to the last st, K1.
Rep row as many times as stated.

Yarn: Aran Weight yarn (for two mats)	
Yarn A Teal	1
Yarn B Light Grey	1
Yarn C White	1

NOTE

If desired, pin out your table mat onto a flat surface to straighten the sides then spray with cold water. Leave to dry completely.

Place mat 1

COLOUR VARIATION 1
(WORKED FROM THE BOTTOM UP)
Using col 1, cast (bind) on 57 sts.
Rows 1-12: Work 12 rows in moss (seed) stitch. Change to col 2.
Row 13: Knit.
Rows 14-24: Work 11 rows in moss (seed)
stitch. Change to col 3.
Row 25: Knit.
Rows 26-36: Work 11 rows in moss (seed) stitch. Change to col 1.
Row 37: Knit.
Rows 38-46: Work 9 rows in moss (seed) stitch. Change to col 2.
Row 47: Knit.
Rows 48-56: Work 9 rows in moss (seed) stitch. Change to col 3.
Row 57: Knit.
Rows 58-66: Work 9 rows in moss (seed) stitch. Change to col 1.
Row 67: Knit.
Rows 68-74: 7 rows in moss (seed) stitch.

To make up
Cast (bind) off purlwise.
Darn in ends.

Place mat 2

COLOUR VARIATION 2
Using col 2, cast (bind) on 57 sts.
Rows 1-12: Work 12 rows in moss (seed) stitch. Change to col 3.
Row 13: Knit.
Rows 14-24: Work 11 rows in moss (seed) stitch. Change to col 1.
Row 25: Knit.
Rows 26-36: Work 11 rows in moss (seed)
stitch. Change to col 2.
Row 37: Knit.
Rows 38-46: Work 9 rows in moss (seed) stitch. Change to col 3.
Row 47: Knit.
Rows 48-56: Work 9 rows in moss (seed) stitch. Change to col 1.
Row 57: Knit.
Rows 58-66: Work 9 rows in moss (seed) stitch. Change to col 2.
Row 67: Knit.
Rows 68-74: 7 rows in moss (seed) stitch.

To make up
Cast (bind) off purlwise.
Darn in ends.

Strap

MAKE ONE PER TABLE MAT
If you wish to make a strap with button hole, you can find the technique needed below.
Using col 3, cast (bind) on 35 sts.
Row 1 (WS): Purl.
Row 2: K3, yo (to create a stitch, which becomes the buttonhole), then k2tog, K to end.
Cast (bind) off.

To make up
Darn in ends.

For each mat:
Roll up your table mat and place the strap around the mat to position the button. Stitch the button in place and fasten the strap around the mat.

Trio of dishcloths

These simple dishcloths make for an achievable first project to learn some basic stitches, and they're great as gifts

What you need

FOR THE SET

In this project we have used 1 x ball of Lily Cotton Sugar'n Cream 100% cotton Aran weight yarn in:

- Colour 1: Robins Egg
- Colour 2: Azalea
- Colour 3: Ecru
- Colour 4: Country Red

Or another equivalent 100% cotton, Aran weight yarn.

- 4mm (US 6) needles
- Yarn needle

FINISHED SIZE

20cm (8in) x 20cm (8in).

TENSION

Work 19 sts and 35 rows in garter stitch to measure 10x10cm/4x4in using 4mm (US 6) needles, or size required to obtain correct tension

Work 18.5 sts and 30 rows in moss stitch to measure 10x10cm/4x4in using 4mm (US 6) needles, or size required to obtain correct tension

Work 19 sts and 29 rows in garter stitch to measure 10x10cm/4x4in using 4mm (US 6) needles, or size required to obtain correct tension.

Although tension is not essential for this project, if you don't match the tension stated your dishcloth may turn out a different size and use a larger amount of yarn.

ABBREVIATIONS

K, knit; **p**, purl; **st(s)**, stitch(es)

Yarn: Lily Cotton Sugar'n Cream, Aran Weight yarn, 100% Cotton (for all three cloths)	
GARTER STITCH: Robins Egg	1
MOSS STITCH: Azalea	1
GARTER RIDGE STRIPED & MOSS STITCH: Ecru	1
GARTER RIDGE STRIPED: Country Red	1

Garter stitch dishcloth

With col 1, cast on 38 sts.
Knit 70 rows or until work meas approx 20cm (8in).
Cast off knitwise.

Moss stitch dishcloth

With col 2, cast on 37 sts.
Row 1: K1, *P1, K1; rep from * to end.
Row 1 forms moss st patt. Cont in moss st for a further 59 rows or until work meas approx 20cm (8in).
Cast off in patt.

Garter ridge striped dishcloth

With col 3, cast on 38 sts.

Rows 1–2: Knit 2 rows with col 4.
Rows 2–4: Knit 2 rows with col 3.
Rows 5–6: Knit 2 rows with col 4.
Change to col 3.
Row 7 (RS): Knit.
Row 8 (WS): K4, P to last 4 sts, K4.
Row 9: Knit.
Row 10: K4, P to last 4 sts, K4.
Change to col 4.
Rows 11–12: Knit 2 rows.
Rows 7–12 set striped pattern with gst border.
Rep Rows 7–12 a further 7 times.
Rows 65–66: Knit 2 rows with col 3.
Rows 67–68: Knit 2 rows with col 4.
Row 69: Knit with col 3.
Cast off knitwise.

NOTE

It is important the yarn you use is 100% cotton for dishcloths, as other fibres will not be suitable. Use a long tail cast on for best results. If preferred, neatly carry yarn up side when knitting the striped dishcloth to save having lots of ends to sew in. You will have enough yarns left over from the striped dishcloth to make another if you reverse the colours for the stripes.

Home | 85

Moss stitch

Pattern by
Donna Jones
Donna Jones designs, edits and teaches handknitting & crochet. She firmly believes creative expression is essential for our well-being and aims to facilitate this in others. Follow Donna's knitterly adventures on
Instagram – @djonesdesigns
www.donnajonesdesigns.co.uk

Garter ridge striped

Garter stitch

To make up

Sew in all remaining ends on wrong side. Although it is not essential to block, if giving as a gift the appearance of your dishcloths will be enhanced if you do so. You can gently block by pinning out flat to dimensions given. Spray liberally with cool water to moisten, patting the water into the knitting until thoroughly dampened. Leave to try dry completely before unpinning.

Home

What you need

FOR THE SET

For this pattern you will need an aran-weighted yarn.
- Texere Wild Silk 8
- Crystal Palace Cotton Chenille
- Rowan Revive DK (doubled)
- Yeoman Yarns Cotton Club No. 6 Aran
- Yeoman Yarns DK Panama (doubled) were used
- 4.5mm (US 7) needles

FINISHED SIZE

Placemat: 32cm (12.5in) deep by 38cm (5in) wide.
Coaster: 10cm (4in) by 10cm (4in).

TENSION

19 stitches and 30 rows = 10cm (4in) in garter stitch.

ABBREVIATIONS

K, knit; **p**, purl; **st(s)**, stitch(es)

Placemat

With colour 1, cast (bind) on 60 stitches.
Work in garter stitch until work measures 38cm (15in) from cast (bind) on edge, bringing in colours 2–7 randomly for whole or part rows.

Cast (bind) off.
Neaten off ends, especially at edges of placemat. Press under a cloth, evening out edges while pressing.

Coaster

With colour 1, cast (bind) on 20 stitches.
Work in garter stitch as for placemat until work measures 10cm (4in) from cast (bind) on edge.
Finish as for placemat.

I-cord coasters

Use this very simple pattern to create cute coasters for your home

What you need

FOR THE SET

For this pattern you shall require Oddments of DK yarn. This is a great way to use up yarn left over from other projects.
- 3.5mm (US 4) 2 x DPNs
- Tapestry needle

FINISHED SIZE

Coaster diameter: 10cm (4in).

TENSION

19 stitches and 30 rows = 10cm (4in) in garter stitch.

ABBREVIATIONS

K, knit; **st(s)**, stitch(es)

Cast (bind) on 4 stitches, leaving a long tail.
K the first row. *While turning the needle holding the sts and the bumps to the back, hold it in your left hand and slide the sts to the other end of the needle.
The yarn should be at the back, but on the furthest st from the end of the tip of the needle. Taking the empty needle, insert it in the first st and with a taut tension, pull the yarn and k the st. K the other 3 sts.
Repeat from * until you have an i-cord measuring 120cm (47in).
Cast (bind) off.

To make up

Starting at the cast (bind) on end of the i-cord, thread the yarn tail onto the tapestry needle. Start to form it into a spiral and start stitching it in place. Gradually spiral and stitch the i-cord until you reach the end. Secure the yarn on the wrong side and tease into a circle shape.

What you need

For this project you will need:
- Approximately 250m (274 yd) of a DK yarn. We used Adriafil, Knitcol in Pascal Fancy
- 4.5mm (US 7) needles
- Tapestry needle

FINISHED SIZE

Cushion covers: 33 x 33cm (13 x 13 in) for a 36 x 36 cm (14 x 14 in) cushion pad.

TENSION

18st and 25 rows = 10cm (4in) in st st using 4.5mm (US 7) needles, or size required in order to obtain the correct tension (gauge).

ABBREVIATIONS

K, knit; **p**, purl

Simple cushion

This stocking stitch cushion project will help you to learn the feel of the yarn and needles

Cast (bind) on 60 stitches.
Row 1 (RS): Knit.
Row 2: Purl.
Repeat these 2 rows until knitting measures
66cm (26in).
Cast (bind) off.

To make up

Darn in all ends. Fold your knitted piece in half lengthways, with right sides facing each other. Sew together the two side edges. Turn the cover right side out, insert the cushion pad and sew the opening closed using mattress stitch.

Gadget cosies

Keep your technology safe in these simple-to-knit cosies

What you need

For this project you will need:
- 1x ball of a DK Yarn. We used Countryside Tweed in Cheviot
- 4mm (US 6) needles
- Tapestry needle

FINISHED SIZE
To fit phone: width 6-8cm (2.5-3in) snuggly.
To fit tablet: To fit tablet width 13-18cm (5-7in) snuggly.

TENSION
29 sts and 28 rows = 10x10cm (4x4in) in rib stitch using 4mm (US 6) needles.

ABBREVIATIONS
K, knit; **p**, purl

Cast (bind) on 32 sts for the smartphone cosy, or 64 sts for the tablet cosy.
Row 1: *Knit 1, purl 1, rep from * to end of row.
Repeat row 1 until knitting measures for your desired length to fit your device.
Cast (bind) off stitches in the K1, P1 rib pattern.

To make up

Darn in ends. Fold knitting in half width-wise and join seams along the cast (bind) on edge, and then down the long side of the cosy. Turn right side out and your cosy is ready to use.

Textured draught excluder

Use moss (seed) stitch to create the textured stripes in this home accessory

Cast (bind) on 50 sts.
Row 1: *K1, P1, rep from *.
Rep row 1 a further 9 times.
**Next row (RS): Knit.
Next row (WS): Purl.
Rep last 2 rows 12 more times ending with RS facing for next row.
Next row: *K1, P1, rep from * to end.
Next row: *P1, K1, rep from * to end.
These 2 rows form the moss (seed) stitch.
Cont in moss (seed) stitch as set for a further 14 rows ending with RS facing for next row **.
Rep between ** and ** twice more.
Next row: Knit.
Next row: Purl.
Rep last 2 rows 12 more times.
Row 1: (K1, P1) to end of row.
Rep row 1 a further 9 times.
Cast (bind) off in rib pattern.

To make up

Darn in ends. With right sides facing, fold the knitting in half lengthways. Join the side edges to create a tube using a mattress stitch. With side edges joined and the draught excluder inside out, flatten the tube, so that the join is in the middle. Now join one of the ribbed openings. Turn out the right way, stuff with preferred material, and close final end by oversewing the seams.

NOTE
If you wish to make a longer draught excluder, work the pattern shown between ** and ** again to add a further 17cm (18in).

Home

What you need

For this pattern you shall require an aran weight yarn. We used:

- 210m (230yd) Sirdar Hayfield Bonus Aran in Petrol
- 5mm (US 8) needles
- Tapestry needle
- Toy stuffing (old tights or old, cut-up t-shirts work equally well)

FINISHED SIZE
To fit standard door width: 66.5cm (26in).

TENSION
Work 18 sts and 22 rows in st st stitch to measure 10x10cm (4x4in) using 5mm (US 8) needles, or the size required to obtain the correct tension.

ABBREVIATIONS
K, knit; **p**, purl; **st(s)**, stitch(es)

Basket stitch container

Whether you need more storage for your yarn, toys or anything else, this basket is perfect – and looks great, too

What you need

For this project use a Cotton DK yarn held double. We used:
- 4 x 50g balls of Debbie Bliss Cotton DK, held double in Stone
- Lining fabric and wadding for sides: 61cm x 16cm
- Lining fabric and wadding for base: 22cm x 22cm
- Yarn needle

FINISHED SIZE
Width: 18cm (7in).
Depth: 13cm (5in).

TENSION
Work 16 sts and 17 rows in pattern to measure 10x10cm using 4.5mm (US 7) needles, or size required to obtain correct tension.

ABBREVIATIONS
St(s), stitch(es); **k**, knit; **p**, purl; **m**, make; **gst**, garter stitch

BASE
Using 4.5mm needles and col 1 held double, cast on 5 sts.
Purl 1 row.
Row 1: K1, M1, K1, M1, K1, M1, K1, M1, K1. (9 sts).
Row 2 and every even row: Purl.
Row 3: K1, (M1, K1) to end. (17 sts).
Row 5: K1, (M1, K2) to end. (25 sts).
Row 7: K1, (M1, K3) to end. (33 sts).
Row 9: K1, (M1, K4) to end. (41 sts).
Row 11: K1, (M1, K5) to end. (49 sts).
Row 13: K1, (M1, K6) to end. (57 sts).
Row 15: K1, (M1, K7) to end. (65 sts).
Row 17: K1, (M1, K8) to end. (73 sts).
Row 19: K1, (M1, K9) to end. (81 sts).
Row 21: K1, (M1, K10) to end. (89 sts).
Row 22: Purl.
Row 23 (WS): Knit to mark edge of base and increase 7 sts evenly across the row (96 sts).

SIDES
Using 4.5mm needles and col 1 held double, cast on 96 sts.
Row 1: (RS): Knit.
Row 2: *K5, P3; rep from * to the end.
Row 3: *K3, P5; rep from * to the end.
Row 4: *K5, P3; rep from * to the end.
Row 5: Knit.
Row 6: K1, P3, *K5, P3; rep from * to the last 4 sts, K4.
Row 7: P4, *K3, P5; rep from * to the last 4 sts, K4.
Row 8: K1, P3, *K5, P3; rep from * to the last 4 sts, K4.
These 8 rows form the pattern. Rep Rows 1-8 until 28 rows have been worked in total (3 repeats of Rows 1-8, then rep Rows 1-4 once more).
Work 3 rows in gst.

HANDLES (MAKE 2)
Using 4.5mm needles and yarn held double, cast on 17 sts.
Rows 1-2: K.
Cast off.

Home | 93

Pattern by
Sian Brown

After doing a Fashion/Textiles BA Sian worked supplying to high street retailers on machine knits. She became interested in handknits and have designed these since, working for magazines, publishers and yarn companies.
www.sianbrown.co.uk

To make up

Pin and sew the base and side seams. Sew on the handles just below the inside top border, opposite each other.

Cut a circle of lining for the base, the size of the base plus 1cm seam allowances (check the measurements of your finished container before cutting the lining. Cut a rectangle of lining for the sides.

Cut the same two pieces in wadding.

Pin the short edges of the side piece together to form a tube. Pin this piece to the circular base. Put inside the container to make sure that it fits. The top should sit just below the beginning of the top border. It is better if the lining is slightly smaller than the knitted piece so that it is eased in to prevent it looking loose or baggy. If it does not fit, pin to the correct size. Sew the side piece together at the short edges. Sew this piece onto the base. Place inside the container, pin and hand sew in place.

Blackberry stitch tea cosy

Brighten up your kitchen with this pretty and practical project. Wrap up your teapot in this textured cosy and keep your tea hot until the very last cup

What you need

For this project we have used Rico Essentials Aran, 50g/85m:
- 2 x 50g balls in Lilac
or an equivelent 100% aran weight yarn in your chosen colour
- 5mm needles
- Yarn needle

FINISHED SIZE
Width: 22cm (8¾in).
Depth: 15cm (6in).

TENSION
20 sts and 20 rows in pattern to measure 10x10cm/4x4in using 5mm needles, or size required to obtain correct tension.

ABBREVIATIONS
St(s), stitch(es); **k**, knit; **p**, purl
P3tog: Purl next 3 stitches together as one stitch – insert right needle purlwise into the next 3 stitches on left needle, purl all 3 stitches together as one stitch (to decrease 2 stitches)
(K1, yrn, K1) into next st: Work all of the instructions within brackets into the next stitch - knit the next stitch but do not take it off the needle, wrap yarn around the needle to make 1 stitch, knit into the same stitch and take it off the needle (increasing 2 stitches)

SIDES (MAKE 2)
Using 5mm needles, cast on 48 sts. Knit 4 rows.

Row 1 (WS): *(K1, yrn, K1) into next st, P3tog; rep from * to end.
Row 2 (RS): *K1, P3; rep from * to end.
Row 3: *K3, P1; rep from * to end.
Row 4: *P1, K3; rep from * to end.
Row 5: *P3tog, (K1, yrn, K1) into next st; rep from * to end.
Row 6: *P3, K1; rep from * to end.
Row 7: *P1, K3; rep from * to end.
Row 8: *K3, P1; rep from * to end.

Repeat these 8 rows until work measures 15cm (6in) from cast on edge, ending with a Row 4 or Row 8.
Next Row (Eyelet Row): K5, (K2tog, yrn, K4) 6 times, K2tog, yrn, K5.
Work 12 rows in gst.
Cast off.

TIE
Cut 8 x 80cm (31 in) lengths of yarn.
Plait/braid to create a tie.
Pin pieces onto your teapot, and mark openings for the handle and spout.
Sew side seams.
Thread tie through eyelets and tie in a bow.

Home | 97

Bobbles tea cosy

It's undoubtedly one of the most rewarding items to knit! Learn how to make the perfect tea cosy, ready to keep your hot drinks hot

What you need

For this project you will require an Aran weight yarn. In the shown example, Drops Alaska and Drops Nepal were used. The Alaska is 100% wool, while the Nepal is 65% wool and 35% alpaca in:

- Off White
- Grey Pink
- Goldenrod
- Light Olive
- Cerise
- 5mm (US 8) needles
- Tapestry needle

FINISHED SIZE

23cmx21cm (9x8in) laid flat.

TENSION

18 sts and 24 rows = 10cm (4in) in stocking stitch .

ABBREVIATIONS

St(s), stitch(es); **k**, knit; **p**, purl; **sl**, slip stitch; **k2tog**, knit 2 stitches together; **psso**, pass slip st over

Yarn: Drops Alaska (100% wool) and Drops Nepal (65% wool and 35% alpaca)	
Yarn A Off White	2
Yarn B Grey Pink	1
Yarn C Goldenrod	1
Yarn D Light Olive	1
Yarn E Cerise	1

Bobbles tea cosy (makes 2 pieces)

With col 1, cast (bind) on 45 sts. Knit 4 rows.
Starting with a purl row, work in stocking stitch until work measures 13cm (5in), adding bobbles in multiple colours randomly, working bobbles on any knit row.

TOP SHAPING

Continuing to add bobbles on knit rows, shape as follows, starting with a knit row.
Row 1 (dec): K7, k2tog *K6, k2tog * work from * to * to last 4 sts, K4 – 40 sts.
Row 2 and every following alternate row: Purl.
Row 3 (dec): K6, k2tog, *K5, k2tog*, work from * to * to last 4 sts, K4 – 35 sts.
Row 5 (dec): K5, k2tog, *K4, k2tog*, work from * to * to last 4 sts, K4 – 30 sts.
Row 7 (dec): K4, k2tog, *K3, k2tog*, work from * to * to last 4 sts, K4 – 25 sts.

Row 9 (dec): K3, k2tog, *K2, k2tog, work from * to * to end – 19 sts.
Row 11 (dec): K2, k2tog, *K1, k2tog,* work from * to * to end – 13 sts.
Row 13 (dec): K2tog to last st, K1 – 7 sts.

Row 15 (dec): Cast off remaining sts.
Rep for second piece.
Press edges under a damp cloth. Pin onto teapot to mark where gaps for handle and spout need to be. Sew up seams, leaving gaps for handle and spout.

POMPOM

Using col 2, make pompom. Trim and sew onto top centre, secure.

TO MAKE THE BOBBLES

K into front, back and front of next st, turn and K3, turn and P3, turn and K3, turn and sl1, k2tog, psso.
On the sample, 16 bobbles in four different colours are worked on each side.

Chevron cushion cover

Simple knit and purl stitches are combined creatively to make this beautiful chevron textured cushion

What you need

For this project you will need to use aran weight yarn in your chosen colour(s). Here we have used Debbie Bliss Falkland Aran, 180m (197yds) per 100g skein; 100% wool in:

- 1 x skein in Duck Egg
- 5mm (US 8) needle
- 40cm x 40cm (15¾in x 15¾in) cushion pad
- 6 x buttons

FINISHED SIZE

40cm x 40cm (15¾in x 15¾in) across, laid flat.

TENSION

18 stitches and 24 rows = 10cm (4in) over stst using 5mm needles, or size required to obtain tension.

ABBREVIATIONS

St(s), stitch(es); **k**, knit; **p**, purl

Cast on 73 sts.
Row 1: K1, *P1, K1; rep from * to end.
Row 1 forms moss stitch pattern.
Repeat this row until 5 rows have been worked.
Beg with a K row, work in st st until work measures 30cm from cast on edge, ending on a RS row.
Next row (WS): K 1 row to mark turn.

FRONT

Row 1 (RS): K1, *P7, K1, rep from * to end.
Row 2: P1, *K7, P1, rep from * to end.
Row 3: K2, *P5, K3, rep from * to last 7 sts, P5, K2.
Row 4: P2, *K5, P3, rep from * to last 7 sts, K5, P2.
Row 5: K3, *P3, K5, rep from * to last 6 sts, P3, K3.
Row 6: P3, *K3, P5, rep from * to last 6 sts, K3, P3.
Row 7: K4, *P1, K7, rep from * to last 5 sts, P1, K4.
Row 8: P4, *K1, P7, rep from * to last 5 sts, K1, P4.
Row 9: As row 2.
Row 10: As Row 1.
Row 11: As Row 4.
Row 12: As Row 3.
Row 13: As Row 6.
Row 14: As Row 5.
Row 15: As Row 8.
Row 16: As Row 7.
These 16 rows set chevron pattern.
Repeat until 96 rows have been worked.
Purl 2 rows to mark turn.

BACK OVELAP

Beg with a K row, work in st st until overlap when folded over sits at the top of the cast on edge (approx 10cm).

NOTE: before starting the moss stitch border, fold this section over. The stitches on the needle should sit just above the cast on edge. If they do not, work further rows until they do.

BUTTONHOLE BAND

Next row: K1, *P1, K1; rep from * to end.
Repeat this row.
Buttonhole row: K5, (k2tog, yo, K10) five times, k2tog, yo, K6.
Next row: K1, *P1, K1; rep from * to end.
Repeat this row.
Cast off.

To make up

Block and press edges. Sew up the side seams. Sew on your chosen buttons.

Home 99

Pattern by
Sian Brown

After doing a Fashion/Textiles BA Sian worked supplying to high street retailers on machine knits. She became interested in handknits and have designed these since, working for magazines, publishers and yarn companies.
www.sianbrown.co.uk

Willowherb lace doily

This unique pattern begins as a square but evolves into a circular shape

What you need

For this project we have used Knit Picks Palette yarn in:
- 1 x ball in Pennyroyal or an equivelent 100% aran weight yarn in your chosen colour
- 3.25mm set of 5 DPNS (US D/3) Alternatively use 4 DPNS, or a 60-80cm long circular needle and magic loop technique if preferred
- Stitch marker
- Crochet hook, 1mm (US 12) or other tool to attach beads, optional
- 88 glass beads, size 6/0 (optional)

FINISHED SIZE
Width: 39cm (15¼in).

TENSION
Tension is not critical for the project but use a relatively loose tension.

Home 101

ABBREVIATIONS

St(s), stitch(es); **k**, knit; **p**, purl; **k2tog**, knit next 2 sts together as one st – insert right needle into the next 3 sts on left needle, knit all 3 sts together as one st the two below are correct and have been copied; **k3tog**, as before, but increase all values by 1; **ssk**, slip slip knit; **(K1, yrn, K1) into next st**, work all the instructions within brackets into the next st – knit the next st but do not take it off the needle, wrap yarn around the needle to make 1 st, knit into the same stitch and take it off the needle (increasing 2 stitches); **Bead (B)**, work a bead into this knit st. If no bead is desired, simply work a knit stitch. Place a bead on your crochet hook. Using the hook in your right hand, lift the st to be worked onto the hook. Catching the st on the hook, use your left hand to slide the bead over the hook and yarn. Remove the st from hook and place it on the left-hand needle. Knit the st with the bead on it; **Quadruple decrease (QD)**, 5 sts will be decreased to just one. Sl 3 sts all together onto your right hand needle. Do NOT slip them one at a time. Join the next 2 sts together by working a k2tog. Carefully lift the 3 sl sts over the k2tog.

Pattern by
Linda Browning
Linda has designed over 50 patterns for magazines, yarn companies, craft books, and most of all, knitters! Many of her patterns feature lace, but she also loves colourwork, cables and beads.
www.tinyknit.com

Using 3.5mm DPNs, cast on 8 sts and distribute evenly on 4 DPNs. Be careful not to twist sts and join in the round.

Rnd 1: Knit all sts.
Rnd 2: (K1, yo) 8 times. (16 sts).
Rnd 3: (K1, yo, K3, yo) 4 times. (24 sts).
Rnd 4: (K1, yo, K5, yo) 4 times. (32 sts).
Rnd 5: (K1, yo, K7, yo) 4 times. (40 sts).
Rnd 6: (K1, yo, K9, yo) 4 times. (48 sts).
Rnd 7: (K1, yo, K11, yo) 4 times. (56 sts).
Rnd 8: (K1, yo, K13, yo) 4 times. (64 sts).
Rnd 9: (K1, yo, K15, yo) 4 times. (72 sts).
Rnd 10: (K1, yo, K17, yo) 4 times. (80 sts).
Rnd 11: (K1, yo, K19, yo) 4 times. (88 sts).
Rnd 12: (K1, yo, K4, P1, K2tog, K3, yo, K1, yo, K3, ssk, P1, K4, yo) 4 times. (96 sts).
Rnds 13, 15, 17, 19: (K6, P1, K5) 8 times.
Round 14: (K2, yo, K2, ssk, P1, K2tog, K2, yo, K1) 8 times.
Round 16: (K3, yo, K1, ssk, P1, K2tog, K1, yo, K2) 8 times.
Round 18: (K4, yo, ssk, P1, K2tog, yo, K3) 8 times.
Round 20: (P1, K2tog, K3, yo, K1, yo, K3, ssk) 8 times.
Rnds 21, 23, 25, 27: (P1, K11) 8 times.
Rnd 22: (P1, k2tog, K2, yo, K3, yo, K2, ssk) 8 times.
Rnd 24: (P1, k2tog, K1, yo, K5, yo, K1, ssk) 8 times.
Rnd 26: (P1, K2tog, yo, K7, yo, ssk) 8 times.
Rnd 28: (K1, yo) to end of round. (192 sts).

NOTE: You may wish to switch to circular needles at this time. Mark the end of round with a stitch marker.

Rnds 29, 31, 33, 35, 37, 39, 41, 43: (K12, P1, K11) 8 times.
Rnd 30: (K2, yo, K1, yo, k 6, sssk, P1, K3tog, K6, yo, K1, yo, K1) 8 times.
Rnd 32: (K3, yo, K1, yo, k 5, sssk, P1, K3tog, K5, yo, K1, yo, K2) 8 times.
Rnd 34: (K4, yo, K1, yo, k 4, sssk, P1, K3tog, K4, yo, K1, yo, K3) 8 times.
Rnd 36: (K5, yo, K1, yo, k 3, sssk, P1, K3tog, K3, yo, K1, yo, K4) 8 times.
Rnd 38: (K6, yo, K1, yo, k 2, sssk, P1, K3tog, K2, yo, K1, yo, K5) 8 times.
Rnd 40: (K7, yo, K1, yo, k 1, sssk, P1, K3tog, K1, yo, K1, yo, K6) 8 times.
Rnd 42: (K8, yo, K1, yo, sssk, P1, K3tog, yo, K1, yo, K7) 8 times.
Rnds 44, 46, 48, 50: (K9, yo, B, yo, QD, yo, B, yo, K8) 8 times.
Rnd 45 and all other odd rounds: Knit all sts.
Rnd 52: (K9, yo, B, yo, QB, yo, B, yo, K8) 8 times.

To make up

Use a very stretchy bind off for this doily. It must be able to be spread out and will be pulled very tightly to show the detailed lace pattern.

After binding off and weaving in all ends, gently wash your doily and blot it dry using absorbent towels. Stretch it out on a blocking surface. Pin the doily out, stretching it as far as possible into the desired shape. Try to even out the shape, so that the yarn overs all line up properly. If you are using cotton thread or yarn, starch will help your doily retain its shape. Allow to dry completely before removing from blocking pad.

Simple baby blankets

The hardest thing will be choosing your favourite from this simple set of blankets

What you need

FOR THE SET

For this project you will need:
- 2 x balls (290m) James C Brett Top Value DK (100% acrylic) in Pink, Blue and Cream
- 4mm (No. 8) knitting needles

FINISHED SIZE

Pink blanket: 80 x 75.5cm (31½ x 29¾in).
Blue blanket: 70 x 70cm (27½ x 27½in).
Cream blanket: 66 x 74cm (26 x 29in).

TENSION

Pink blanket: 25 stitches and 30 rows, to 10 x 10cm, over pattern, using 4mm needles.

Blue and cream blankets: 22 stitches and 28 rows, to 10 x 10cm, over stocking stitch, using 4mm needles.

ABBREVIATIONS

St(s), stitch(es); **k**, knit; **p**, purl; **yf**, yarn forward (to make 1 st); **k2tog**, knit 2 sts together (to decrease 1 st); **skpo**, slip 1 st, knit 1 st, pass the slipped st over the knitted st (to decrease 1 st)

Yarn: James C Brett Top Value DK (100% acrylic) (balls) 290m	
Pink (8421)	2
Blue (8418)	2
Cream (0844)	2

Pink blanket

With 4mm needles and Pink, cast on 202 sts.
K 3 rows.
Continue in pattern as follows:
1st row: K3, [k1, yf, k4, k2tog, skpo, k4, yf] to last 4 sts, k4.
2nd row: K3, p to last 3 sts, k3.
These 2 rows form the pattern.
Pattern until work measures approximately 75cm, ending after 1st row.
K 2 rows. Cast off.

Blue blanket

With 4mm needles and Blue, cast on 154 sts.
1st row: K2, [p2, k2] to end.
2nd row: P2, [k2, p2] to end.
3rd row: P2, [k2, p2] to end.
4th row: K2, [p2, k2] to end.
These 4 rows form double moss-st pattern.

Pattern until work measures approximately 70cm, ending after 1st or 3rd row.
Cast off.

Cream blanket

With 4mm needles and Cream, cast on 146 sts.
K 5 rows.
Continue in pattern as follows:
1st row: K to end.
2nd row: K4, p to last 4 sts, k4.
Repeat these 2 rows, 9 times more.
21st row: K4, p to last 4 sts, k4.
22nd row: K to end.
Repeat these 2 rows, 9 times more.
These last 40 rows form the pattern.
Work straight until work measures approximately 73cm, ending after a 20th or 40th row.
K 5 rows. Cast off.

For all blankets: Press according to yarn band.

NOTE

Blankets are reversible. Yarn amounts are based on average requirements and are approximate. Instructions in square brackets are worked as stated after 2nd bracket.

Quick & Easy KNITTING

Strawberry pie blanket

This knitted quilt is about everything one calls sweet home – cosiness, warmth, and the smell of a freshly baked strawberry pie

What you need

FOR THE SET

In this project we have used a variety of aran/chunky yarns (see table).

- Each square requires approx 14g of yarn
- 7mm needles
- Cable needle (optional)
- Tapestry needle
- Scissors

FINISHED SIZE

90x90cm (35½x35½in). Each square is approx. 13x13cm (5x5in). Each square requires approx 14g of yarn.

TENSION

Work 14 sts and 20 rows in garter stitch (blocked) to measure 10x10cm/4x4in using 7mm (US 10½ or US 11) needles, or size required to obtain correct tension.

Tension is not critical and can be changed to fit the desired yarn.

ABBREVIATIONS

St(s), stitch(es); **k**, knit; **p**, purl; **sl**, slip stitch; **k2tog**, knit 2 stitches together; **p2tog**, purl 2 stitches together

Yarn: Rowan Pure Wool Worsted (100% wool; 100g/200m) ball(s) using 2 strands held together throughout.	
Yarn A Pink	2
Yarn B Cream	1
Yarn: Art Merino De Luxe 50 (50% wool, 50% acrylic; 100g/280m) ball(s) using 3 strands held together throughout.	
Yarn A Ivory	2
Yarn B Baby Pink	2
Yarn: Art Merino Bulky (30% wool, 70% acrylic; 100g/100m) Ball(s)	
Yarn A Beige	1
Yarn B Sand	1

STRIP COMPOSITION

Create each strip as follows:
square 1
Cast on 17 sts.
Rows 1–24: Knit using any Square Pattern of your choice. Stop after completing the WS row.
Cut the yarn and attach the new colour.

SQUARE 2

Rows 1–24: Knit using any Square Pattern of your choice. Stop after completing the WS row.
Cut the yarn and attach the new colour.
Follow the same instructions as given for Square 2, for the next 4 squares.

SQUARE 7

Rows 1–24: Knit using any Square Pattern of your choice. Stop after completing the WS row.
Row 25 (RS): Cast off as follows: K1, (slip st back to left needle, K2tog) until 1 stitch is left.
Cut yarn leaving approx 20cm (8in) and pull it through the loop of the last stitch.

Tip

The pattern is great for using leftover yarn as well as for knitting up those oddments from your stash.

NOTE

The blanket is knitted as 7 vertical strips of 7 squares, which are later sewn together. The neat braid-like edge of the squares is created by slipping first stitches. Sl 1 wyib if the first facing stitch is knitted; sl 1 wyif if the first facing stitch is purled.

Each square is 17 sts wide and 24 rows high. The number of completed squares can be changed depending on the yarn/tension/desired size of your blanket.

Quick & Easy KNITTING

SQUARES

Garter

Row 1 (RS): Sl 1, knit until the end of the row.

Rows 2–24: Rep Row 1 another 23 times.

Seed (British moss)

Row 1 (RS): Sl 1, knit until the end of the row.

Row 2 (WS): Sl 1, (K1, P1) until the end of the row.

Rows 3–24: Rep Row 2 another 22 times.

Broken rib

Row 1 (RS): Sl 1, knit until the end of the row.

Row 2 (WS): Sl 1, (P1, K1) until the end of the row.

Rows 3–24: Rep Rows 1–2 another 11 times.

Corn (same as WS of broken rib)

Row 1 (RS): Sl 1, knit until the end of the row.

Row 2 (WS): As Row 1.

Row 3: Sl 1, (K1, P1) until the end of the row.

Rows 4–23: Rep Rows 2–3 another 10 times.

Row 24: As Row 1.

Balustrade

Row 1 (RS): Sl 1, knit until the end of the row.

Row 2 (WS): As Row 1.

Row 3: Sl 1, (K1, P1) until the end of the row.

Row 4: Sl 1, (P1, K1) until the end of the row.

Row 5: As Row 3.

Row 6: Sl 1, knit until the end of the row.

Rows 7–24: Repeat Rows 1–6 another 3 times.

Basketweave

Row 1 (RS): Sl 1, knit until the end of the row.

Row 2 (WS): Sl 1, (P2, K4) twice, P2, K2.

Row 3: Sl 1, P1, (K2, P4) twice, K2, P1.

Row 4: Sl 1, purl until the end of the row.

Row 5: Sl 1, (P4, K2) twice, P4.

Row 6: Sl 1, K3, (P2, K4) twice, K1.

Rows 7–24: Rep Rows 1–6 another 4 times.

Double moss (Little check)

Row 1 (RS): Sl 1, knit until the end of the row.

Row 2 (WS): Sl 1, (P2, K2) until the end of the row.

Row 3: Sl 1, P1, (K2, P2) 3 times, K2, P1.

Row 4: Sl 1, (K2, P2) until the end of the row.

Row 5: Sl 1, K1, (P2, K2) 3 times, P2, K1.

Rows 6–21: Rep Rows 2–5 another 4 times.

Row 22: As Row 2.

Row 23: As Row 3.

Row 24: As Row 4.

Gear

Row 1 (RS): Sl 1, knit until the end of the row.

Row 2 (WS): Sl 1, P1, K2, P1, K2, P3, K2, P1, K2, P2.

Row 3: Sl 1, K1, P2, K1, P2, K3, P2, K1, P2, K2.

Row 4: As Row 2.

Row 5: Sl 1, P2, K3, P2, K1, P2, K3, P2, K1.

Row 6: Sl 1, K2, P3, K2, P1, K2, P3, K2, P1.

Row 7: As Row 5.

Row 8: As Row 6.

Row 9: Sl 1, K1, P2, K1, P2, K3, P2, K1, P2, K2.

Row 10–17: Rep Rows 2–9 once more.

Rows 18–24: Repeat Rows 2–8 once.

Honeycomb

Row 1 (RS): Sl 1, knit until last 2 sts, Kfb, K1. (18 sts).

Row 2 (WS): Sl 1, purl until the end of the row.

Row 3: Sl 1, (C2B, C2F) until the last st, K1.

Row 4: As Row 2.

Row 5: Sl 1, (C2F, C2B) until the last st, K1.

Rows 6–21: Rep Rows 2–5 another 4 times.

Row 22: As Row 2

Row 23: As Row 3

Row 24: Sl 1, P2tog, purl until the end of the row. (17 sts).

SQUARES ORDER

STRIP 1 (from the bottom up, pattern/ colour): Balustrade/pink, Garter/ cream, Broken Rib/beige, Seed/ivory, Balustrade/pink, Basketweave/cream, Gear/beige.

STRIP 2: Corn/sand, Double Moss/baby pink, Basketweave/ivory, Garter/pink, Corn/sand, Honeycomb/baby pink, Double Moss/ivory

STRIP 3: Honeycomb/baby pink, Seed/ ivory, Balustrade/beige, Gear/baby pink, Basketweave/cream, Seed/ cocoa, Broken Rib/pink

STRIP 4: Corn/cream, Gear/sand, Double Moss/pink, Seed/ivory, Broken Rib/sand, Basketweave/baby pink, Garter/ivory

STRIP 5: Broken Rib/cocoa, Garter/ baby pink, Corn/ivory, Balustrade/ sand, Honeycomb/pink, Double Moss/ ivory, Gear/baby pink

STRIP 6: Seed/pink, Basketweave/ivory, Honeycomb/beige, Corn/baby pink, Garter/cream, Balustrade/pink, Double Moss/sand

STRIP 7: Double Moss/ivory, Corn/sand, Garter/pink, Gear/cream, Broken Rib/ beige, Seed/ivory, Corn/baby pink.

To make up

Block or steam the stripes into shape. Sew them together. Weave in ends.

Holidays
PATTERNS

110
Tilia Heart

112
Little carrot pouch

114
Easter egg decorations

116
Pumpkin place-holder

118
Snowflake cushion cover

120
Chunky cabled wreath

Tilia Heart

The perfect gift for Valentine's Day, or even a just-because day

What you need

For this project you will need:
- Any double-knit yarn scraps (approx. 18m/20yrd)
- 3mm double pointed needles (at least 15cm/6in long)
- Large-eyed needle for sewing up & weaving in ends
- Small amount of toy stuffing

FINISHED SIZE
7–8cm wide.

TENSION
Tension is not critical for this project.

ABBREVIATIONS
k, knit, **p,** purl, **St(s),** stitch(es); **kfb,** make a stitch by knitting into the front and back of the stitch, **k2tog,** knit 2 together, **ssk,** slip 2 stitches knit-wise onto right needle then knit together through the back of the loops

NOTE
The heart shape is knitted flat, in one piece. It's a quick knit with very little sewing up. Double-pointed needles are essential as you will be turning the work.

This pattern has been written for double knit (DK) yarn but can easily be adapted for most yarns by using needles a few sizes smaller than stated on the yarn band. The aim is for the fabric to have quite a close weave, so the stuffing doesn't show.

The purl stitch in the middle of the work acts as a centre marker and also makes it easy to fold the finished piece.

The piece is knitted from the bottom up, creating the heart body then 3 lobes (see figs 1 to 4).

HEART BODY
Cast on 7 stitches
Row 1: p3, k1 (this is the centre stitch), p3 (wrong side)
Row 2: kfb, k1, kfb, p1 (centre stitch), kfb, k1, kfb (11 sts, right side)
Row 3: p5, k1, p5
Row 4: k2, kfb, kfb, k1, p1, k1, kfb, kfb, k2 (15 sts)
Row 5: p7, k1, p7
Rows 6–20:
Right side rows: k2, kfb, k to 2 sts before centre stitch, kfb, k1, p1, k1, kfb, k to last 3 sts, kfb, k1
Wrong side rows: p to centre stitch, k1, purl to end
You should now have 43 stitches.
Row 21: k to centre stitch, p1, k to end

FIRST LOBE
p11, turn
k11, turn
p11, turn
k1, k2tog, ssk, k1, k2tog, ssk, k1 (7 sts)
Cut the yarn approx. 15cm/6in and pull through the 7 stitches

SECOND LOBE
This lobe is larger than the other two as it's both the front and back knitted as one.
Re-join the yarn, p10, k1, p10, turn
k10, p1, k10, turn
p10, k1, p10, turn
k1, k2tog, ssk, k1, k2tog, ssk, p1, k2tog, ssk, k1, k2tog, ssk, k1 (13 sts)
Cut the yarn to a length suitable for sewing up the heart at the end, pull through the 13 sts.

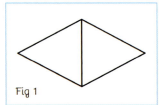
Fig 1

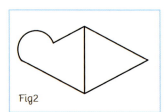
Fig 2

Fig 3

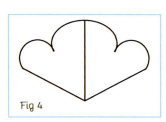
Fig 4

Holidays | 111

THIRD LOBE
Re-join the yarn, p11, turn
k11, turn
p11, turn
k1, k2tog, ssk, k1, k2tog, ssk, k1 (7 sts)
Cut the yarn approx. 15cm (6in) and pull through the 7 sts

To make up
Secure ends and sew up the heart leaving a gap to add stuffing. Lightly stuff the heart then stitch the gap closed. Shape gently.

Pattern by
Emma Sadler
Emma is the crafter behind Fallen Leaf Makes, where she shares her love of knitting, embroidery and textile jewellery. She can also be found on Instagram and Ravelry.
www.facebook.com/ fallenleafmakes

Little carrot pouch

The perfect way to hold all those Easter treats

What you need

For this project you will need Any orange and green worsted weight yarn can be used, which make this project a great scrap buster.

- Each carrot takes approximately 20-25 yards of yarn total
- US #7 (4.5mm) straight knitting needles
- Scissors
- Tapestry Needle
- I (5.50 mm) crochet hook

FINISHED SIZE

7 in. long x 2 ¾ in. wide at the top.

TENSION

Work 16 sts and 17 rows in pattern to measure 10x10cm using 4.5mm (US 7) needles, or size required to obtain correct tension.

ABBREVIATIONS

St(s), stitch(es); **K**, Knit, **yo**, yarn over; **Kf&b**, knit into the front and back of the same stitch; **K2tog**, knit 2 stitches together

---

With orange, cast on 5 sts.

Row 1: Purl
Row 2: Knit
Row 3: Purl
Row 4: Kf&b, knit to the last stitch, Kf&b (7 sts.)
Rows 5-36: Repeat rows 1-4 until you have 23 sts. on your needle
Row 37: Purl

Change to green

Row 38: K1, (yo, K2tog) repeat to the end of the row (23 sts.)
Row 39: Purl
Row 40: Knit
Row 41: Purl
Row 42: Knit
Row 43: Purl
Bind off

To make up

Fold the carrot in half with the stockinette side in and seam down the side. Weave in ends and turn right side out.
To make the drawstring, crochet a 12-inch chain. Weave the chain through the eyelet holes and knot at the end. You could also substitute an i-cord or ribbon for the drawstring.

NOTE

Carrot is knit from the bottom up in one piece and seamed together.

Easter egg decorations

Bring some colour to your Easter celebrations with these knitted eggs

What you need

For this project you will need any DK yarn (or any yarn – the thicker your yarn, the bigger your eggs will be).

- Needles: US 3 / UK 10 / 3.25mm – either double-pointed or circular at least 60cm- (23in-) long for magic loop (or needles to suit your yarn; perhaps drop a size to ensure a dense fabric for stuffing)
- Toy stuffing or a real egg!

FINISHED SIZE
Length: 6cm (2.5in).
Circumference: 11.5cm (4.5in).

TENSION
22 stitches and 36 rows, to 10 x 10cm, over pattern, using 4mm needles.

ABBREVIATIONS
St(s), stitches; **k**, knit; **p**, purl; **st(s)**, stitch(es); **k2tog**, knit two stitches together

BOTTOM SECTION (INCREASES)

Cast on 6, divide onto DPNs/magic loop and join in the round
Row 1: Knit, increasing 6, ie in every stitch (12 sts) (giving you 2 sts per segment)
Row 2: Knit
Row 3: Knit, increasing 6 (18 sts) (3 sts per segment)
Row 4: Knit
Row 5: Knit, increasing 6 (24 sts) (4 sts per segment)
Row 6: Knit
Row 7: Knit, increasing 6 (30 sts) (5 sts per segment)
Row 8: Knit

MIDDLE SECTION

NOTE: Add pattern or stripes if desired – see charts on opposite page
Rows 9-16: Knit 8 rows

TOP SECTION (DECREASES)

Row 17: Knit, decreasing 6 (24 sts) (4 sts per segment)
Rows 18-20: Knit 3 rows
Row 21: Knit, decreasing 6 (18 sts) (3 sts per segment)

Pause to sew in any ends (especially from other colours in middle section pattern band) and stuff the egg.

Rows 22-23: Knit 2 rows
Row 24: Knit, decreasing 6 (12 sts) (2 sts per segment)
Row 25: Knit, decreasing 6, K2tog on every stitch (6 sts)

Cut yarn and pull tail through stitches, finish stuffing if using toy stuffing, gather up tight and sew in the loose end.

NOTE

Each egg starts and finishes the same, but there are a variety of options for the 'flat' section in the middle between the increases and decreases. These are presented as coloured charts for ease.

All knitting is in the round on magic loop or double-pointed needles, in stocking stitch, ie all rows knitted, except where explicitly stated.

Holidays

Egg Middle Section Charts

All charts below are for the whole width of the egg (30 sts). On all charts, begin at the bottom and knit from right to left, i.e. as if you're looking at the knitting.

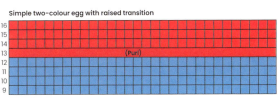

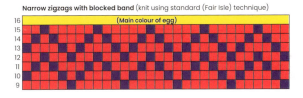

To make up

Filling with a solid egg gives a far better, defined shape than toy stuffing, but it can be a little tricky knitting around the top of it. It helps to pull up your knitting as far as you can, and after a couple of rows it should get easier. You may also find it easier to switch to circular needles with shorter straight sections, or double-pointed needles.

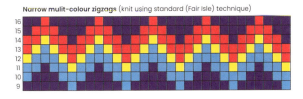

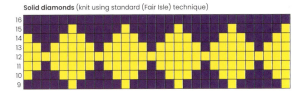

Pattern by
Anna Funnell

Anna Funnell is the owner of WombleKnits. She hates waste and loves putting her knitting skills to use creating easy, practical, eco-friendly designs for reusable items, using sustainable yarns.
www.wombleknits.com

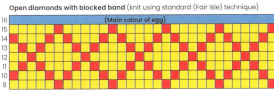

Stranded/Fair Isle colourwork

In the 'flat', patterned section of each egg (except the simple two-colour egg) you will be knitting with two to three colours at once. When switching to a new colour, you will need to wrap it over and around the previous colour to avoid leaving a gap.

Pumpkin place-holder

Direct your guests to their place at the Halloween party table with a mini knitted and felted pumpkin

What you need

For this project you will need Rowan, Scottish Tweed Aran 100g (170m) ball in:
- Rust (009)
- Stitch marker
- Hollowfibre toy stuffing
- Strong orange sewing thread and needle
- Green felt fabric
- Sequins and beads to embellish
- 20cm (8in) length copper wire

TENSION
Tension is not critical for this project.

ABBREVIATIONS
St(s), stitches; **k**, knit; **p**, purl; **inc**, increase; **k2tog**, knit two stitches together

---

Cast on 16 sts and divide between the 4mm double pointed needles.
Round 1: *K1, P1; rep from * to end.
Round 2: *Inc 1, P1; rep from * to end. [24 sts]
Round 3: *K2, P1; rep from * to end.
Round 4: *Inc 1, K1, P1; rep from * to end. [32 sts]
Round 5: *K3, P1; rep from * to end.
Round 6: *Inc 1, K2, P1; rep from * to end. [40 sts]
Round 7: *K4, P1; rep from * to end.
Round 8: *Inc 1, K3, P1; rep from * to end. [48 sts]
Round 9: *K5, P1; rep from * to end.
Round 10: *Inc 1, K4, P1; rep from * to end. [56 sts]
Round 11: *K6, P1; rep from * to end.
Round 12: *K6, Inc 1 purlwise; rep from * to end. [64 sts]
Round 13: *K6, P2; rep from * to end.
Work round 13 eight times more

SHAPE TOP
Round 1: *K6, p2tog; rep from * to end. [56 sts]
Round 2: *K6, P1; rep from * to end.
Round 3: *K4, k2tog, P1; rep from * to end. [48 sts]
Round 4: *K5, P1; rep from * to end.
Round 5: *K3, k2tog, P1; rep from * to end. [40 sts]
Round 6: *K4, P1; rep from * to end.
Round 7: *K2, k2tog, P1; rep from * to end. [32 sts]
Round 8: *K3, P1; rep from * to end.
Round 9: *K1, k2tog, P1; rep from * to end. [24 sts]
Round 10: *K2, P1; rep from * to end.
Round 11: *K2tog, P1; rep from * to end. [16 sts]
Round 12: *K1, P1; rep from * to end.
Round 13: *K2tog; rep from * to end. [8 sts]

Break yarn and thread through rem 8 sts.

Tip
This makes the ideal first project to try your hand at felting. Simply follow our easy instructions and you'll see how your knitted yarn fuses together.

Holidays

To make up

Felt the pumpkin by agitating in very hot soapy water until the fibres begin to fuse and matt. Stuff the pumpkin very firmly using toy stuffing.

Using a double length of strong thread, darn up the small hole at the base of the pumpkin and then work several long stitches from base to top point of pumpkin, drawing up tight to create a dimple in the pumpkin.

Cut a leaf from the green felt fabric and embellish with sequins (if desired) and stitch into place at the top of the pumpkin.

Make the card holder by wrapping the length of copper wire twice around the handle of a wooden spoon and then twisting the two ends together, working from the middle point of the wire.

Push the twisted ends of the wire into the top of the pumpkin and slot the name card between the two loops of wire that are left at the top.

Snowflake cushion cover

Bring a winter flourish to your sofa this year with this easy to follow snowflake chart cushion

Yarn: Designer Yarns DY Choice Aran With Wool (75% acrylic, 25% wool) 200m per 100g ball(s).

Yarn A Cranberry	2
Yarn B Ecru	1

Holidays

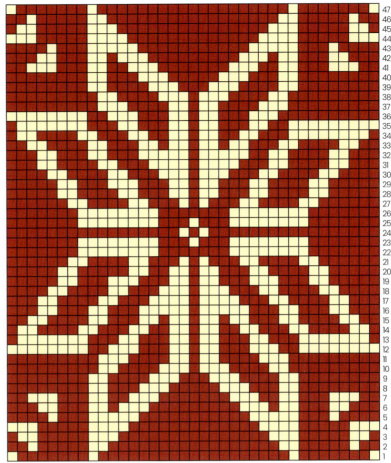

Pattern chart Yarn A: ■ Yarn B: ☐

What you need

For this project use an aran weight yarn, we used Designer Yarns DY Choice Aran With Wool in:
- Cranberry
- Ecru
- 4.5mm (US 7) Needles
- 40cm x 40 cm cushion pad
- 6 buttons
- Yarn needle

FINISHED SIZE

Approximately 38cm x 38cm to snugly fit cushion insert 40cm x 40 cm.

TENSION

17 sts and 24 rows = 10cm (4in) over st st using 4.5mm needles.

ABBREVIATIONS

Amend St(s), stitch(es); **k**, knit; **p**, purl; **k2tog**, knit two sts together

Made in 1 piece

BACK

With col 2, cast on 72 sts.
Row 1: (K1, P1) to end.
Row 2: (P1, K1) to end.
These 2 rows form moss st patt. Work 3 rows more in patt.
Change to col 1.
Beg with a K row, work in st st, until work measures 30 cm from the cast on edge, ending with a K row.
Next Row (WS): Knit, making garter ridge.

FRONT

Work 20 rows in st st, inc 1 st on the first row. 73 sts
Start chart.
Row 1: K18, K37 sts of chart row 1, K18.
Row 2: P18, P37 sts of chart row 2, P18.
Cont the chart, working 18 sts before and after the chart on each row, until all 47 rows have been worked.
Beg with a P row work 20 rows in st st, dec 1 st at the end of the last row and ending with a P row. (72 sts)
Next Row (RS): Purl, making garter ridge.

OVERLAP

Beg with a P row cont in st st until overlap measures 10cm, ending with a P row.
Fold over to the back, and check that the last row on the needles sits just above the cast on edge. If it does not, adjust so that it does.
Change to col 2.
K 1 row.
Row 1: (K1, P1) to end.

NOTE

When working from the chart, right side rows are knitted and worked from right to left. Wrong side rows are purled and worked from left to right.

Row 2: (P1, K1) to end.
Row 3 (eyelet row): K5, (k2tog, yo, K10) 5 times, k2tog, yo, K5.
Row 4: (K1, P1) to end.
Row 5: (P1, K1) to end.
Cast off.

To make up

Weave in ends.
Block and press to the correct measurements.
Pin and sew the side seams.
Sew on the buttons to correspond with the buttonholes.

Quick & Easy KNITTING

Chunky cabled wreath

Quick and easy to make, this pretty wreath uses chunky yarn to create a textured Christmas decoration that can be embellished or left plain

What you need

In this project we have used Drops Eskimo, 50m per 50g ball; 100% wool. You will need to use a equivalent, chunky weight yarn in your chosen colour.

- 6.5mm (US 10 ½) needles
- 7mm needles
- Cable needle
- A selection of felted balls or 4-6mm beads
- Yarn needle
- Scissors

FINISHED SIZE
To fit a wreath that is 25cm across.

TENSION
Tension is not critical – just make sure that your knitted piece measures approximately 15cm (6in) wide and will fit around the ring when slightly stretched.

ABBREVIATIONS
St(s), stitch(es); **k**, knit; **p**, purl; **C4F**, cable 4 front – slip next 2 stitches on a cable needle and hold at front of work, knit next 2 stitches from left needle, knit 2 stitches from cable needle

Yarn: Drops Eskimo, 50m per 50g ball; 100% wool. Ball(s).	
Light Green, sh 35	2

Using 6.5mm needles, cast on 20 sts.
Row 1 (RS): K7, P1, K4, P1, K7.
Row 2: P7, K1, P4, K1, P7.
Row 3: As Row 1.
Row 4: As Row 2.
Row 5: K7, P1, C4F, P1, K7.

Row 6: As Row 2.
Rows 1-6 form the pattern. Rep Rows 1-6 until your piece, when slightly stretched, will fit around the wreath. Cast off.

To make up

First, sew the cast on and cast off edges together using mattress stitch for a flat seam.
Place the knitted piece around the wreath and bring the long edges together. Slip stitch or mattress stitch the long edges together, and make sure that the seam sits at the back of the wreath.

Wrap a short length of ribbon once around the seam to cover and slip stitch in place. Make a hanging loop of approximately 5cm (2in) and slip stitch the end of the ribbon to the back of the wreath. Make a bow from a shorter length of ribbon and sew it in place at the front of the ribbon loop.

If desired, add beads or felted balls to the centre of every alternate cable.

Pattern by
Lynne Rowe
Lynne Rowe is a knit and crochet designer, technical editor, craft author and tutor. She loves to pass on her skills to help others to knit, crochet and create.
www.thewoolnest.blogspot.co.uk. & www.knitcrochetcreate.com

Holidays | 121

Reference

124
Yarns

126
Knitting needles

128
Knitting kit bag

130
Yarn labels

131
Choosing yarn colours

132
Knitting abbreviations

133
Stitch symbol charts

134
Stitch patterns

139
Glossary

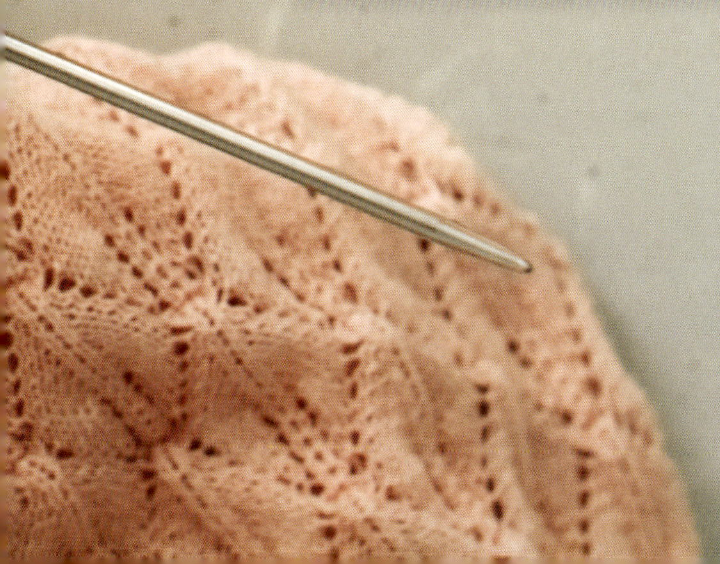

Yarns

To begin knitting, it's pretty straightforward, as all you need are two things: a pair of knitting needles and a ball of yarn. The yarn that you decide to use will play a part in determining which needles you work with, so let's start by looking at the many types of yarn available to you.

Yarns are made with a wide variety of fibres; most are natural, some are synthetic, and others blend different fibres together. All yarns have different textures and properties, and will affect the look and feel of your finished project. For example, wool is stretchy and tough, alpaca is soft and luxurious, and natural and synthetic blends are durable with other enhanced properties.

When choosing a yarn you also need to consider its thickness, usually called its weight. Different weights affect the appearance of your project and the number of stitches needed.

When learning to knit, it's a good idea to start with a medium-weight yarn that feels comfortable in your hand and is smooth but not too slippery. A yarn described as worsted, Aran or 10-ply in wool or a wool blend is ideal.

Wool
Wool is very warm and tough, which makes it great for winter wear. It can be fine and soft or rough and scratchy, but will soften with washing. It's mostly affordable, durable and a good choice for the new knitter.

Cotton
This natural vegetable fibre is typically less elastic than wool, and is known for its robustness and washability. Cotton has a lovely stitch definition when knitted, and is good for homewares and bags. However, it can be a bit hard on the hands.

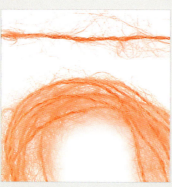

Mohair
Mohair is a silk-like fibre that comes from the Angora goat. It's a yarn that dyes particularly well and is commonly blended with other fibres. It makes for fantastic winter garments as it is warm and durable.

Acrylic
Made from polyacrylonitrile, acrylic yarn is both affordable and also washable. This synthetic yarn is very soft to the touch and comes in a wide variety of colours and textures. Acrylic is commonly blended with other yarns in order to add durability.

Alpaca
With long and fine fibres, alpaca yarn can sometimes be hairy looking, but it is one of the warmest and most luxurious wools out there. It is also incredibly soft, and comes in varieties such as baby and royal, which are even softer.

Natural and synthetic blends
Blending natural and man-made fibres often creates yarns that are stronger and more versatile. It can also enhance their appearance, making them shinier or more vibrant. Blended yarns are often washable, making them great for garments for children.

Did you know?
Every ball of yarn comes with a recommended needle size, which is printed on the label. Use bigger needles than this to make a more open stitch, and smaller ones to make a tighter, more compact fabric.

Yarn weights

Type	Properties	Ideal for	Metric	US	Old UK
Lace, 2-ply, fingering	Extremely light, lace yarn produces a very delicate texture on 2mm (US 0) hooks. Bigger needles will produce a more open fabric.	Lace	2mm 2.25mm 2.5mm	0 1	14 13
Superfine, 3-ply, fingering, baby	Using very slim needles, superfine yarn is perfect for lightweight, intricate lace work.	Finely woven socks, shawls, babywear	2.75mm 3mm 3.25mm	2 3	12 11 10
Fine, 4-ply, sport, baby	Fine yarn is great for socks, and can also be used in items that feature slightly more delicate textures.	Light jumpers, babywear, socks, accessories	3.5mm 3.75mm 4mm	4 5 6	9 8
Double knit (DK), light worsted, 5/6-ply	An extremely versatile weight yarn, DK can be used to create a wide variety of items and crochets up relatively quickly.	Jumpers, light-weight scarves, blankets, toys	4mm 4.5mm	7	7
Aran, medium worsted, Afghan, 12-ply	With many yarns in this thickness using a variety of fibres to make them machine washable, aran yarn is good for garments with thick cabled detail and functional items.	Jumpers, cabled garments, blankets, hats, scarves, mittens	5mm 5.5mm	8 9	6 5
Chunky, bulky, craft, rug, 14-ply	Quick to crochet, chunky yarn is perfect for warm outerwear. Often made from lightweight fibres to prevent drooping.	Rugs, jackets, blankets, hats, legwarmers, winter accessories	6mm 6.5mm 7mm 8mm	10 10.5 11	4 3 2 0
Super chunky, super bulky, bulky, roving, 16-ply and upwards	Commonly used with very large needles, super chunky yarn crochets up very quickly. Large stitches make mistakes easy to spot.	Heavy blankets, rugs, thick scarves	9mm 10mm	13 15	00 000

Recommended Needle Sizes

Knitting needles

Knitting needles come in many types, sizes and materials. Once you become more familiar with knitting, you may find that you prefer one type over another, but the variations are designed with different patterns and yarns in mind. This guide will explain the features of each, but the best way to decide which needles suit you is to practise and find the ones that feel most comfortable.

Learning to knit on bent, dull or rough needles will be a frustrating process, so it's worth investing in a good pair that feel nice in your hands to get started. To practise knitting, it's better to work with thick yarn as this will make it easier to spot mistakes. If you're getting started with yarn that is Aran weight or thicker, your first pair of needles should be at least 5mm (US 8) in diameter.

Straight needles
Pointed at one end with a stopper at the other, straight knitting needles come in pairs and a variety of lengths. Short needles are best for small projects and long needles are recommended for wider projects, such as blankets. When you're new to knitting, it's best to start with long, straight needles, as they have more length to hold on to and give the most support to the hand.

Metal needles
Strong and not prone to bending, metal needles are good for all types of yarns, especially wool, wool blends and acrylic. Stitches move quickly on the polished surface of metal needles, which makes them quick to knit with but also unsuitable for beginners, as stitches can easily slip off the needle's tip. Metal needles of more than 8mm (US 11) in diameter can be heavy and difficult to work with.

Plastic needles
Lightweight and flexible, plastic needles can be used with all types of yarns. The smooth surface of plastic needles allows stitches to move quickly, but not as quickly as on metal needles, so the risk of stitches slipping off the needle is reduced. Larger needles are commonly made of plastic in order to reduce their weight.

Bamboo needles
Bamboo needles are strong and tend to be lighter than metal needles. The bamboo has a slight grip, which helps to keep stitches regularly spaced, creating an even knit. This also minimises the risk of stitches slipping off the needle's tip, making them an excellent choice for beginners. Bamboo needles are also recommended for arthritis sufferers, as they are warm to the touch and can warp slightly to fit the curvature of the hand.

Reference

Square needles
Although most needles are cylindrical, square needles with four flat sides make a more consistent stitch and require less hand tension to maintain in position. This makes them good for beginners and arthritis sufferers.

Double-pointed and circular needles
In order to produce a tube of knitting without a seam, such as a sock or cowl, you will need to knit in the round using double-pointed or circular needles. Choosing which to use will often depend on the length of your project. Double-pointed needles (DPNs) can knit a very narrow tube, whereas circular needles are better for larger projects.

Double-pointed needles
Usually sold in sets of four or five, double-pointed needles (DPNs) have points at both ends. They are typically quite short and do not hold a lot of stitches, so are best for smaller projects, such as socks.

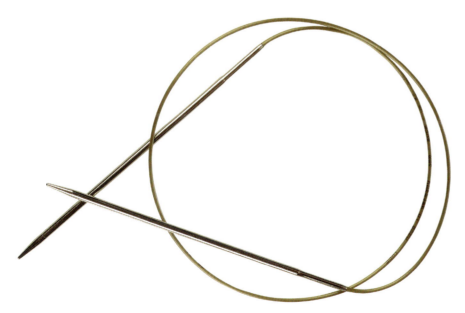

Circular needles
These are two straight needles connected with a flexible plastic cord. The cord can come in many different lengths, from 30-152cm (12-60in), and it is important to choose a length that is appropriate for your project. A good rule of thumb is to use a cord that will match or be slightly smaller than the circumference of the piece you are knitting.

Size
Knitting needles come in a variety of diameters, from as small as 1.5mm (US 000 / 00) up to 25mm (US 50). The size of the needle that you use will determine the size of the stitch you create, and most yarns will come with a recommended needle size.

There are three common needle-sizing systems: European metric, old British and American. Use this chart to convert between sizes. If your needles are not labelled by diameter, you may need to buy a needle size gauge to establish their size.

Metric (mm)	US	Old UK
1.5	000/00	N/A
2	0	14
2.25 / 2.5	1	13
2.75	2	12
3	N/A	11
3.25	3	10
3.5	4	N/A
3.75	5	9
4	5	8
4.5	7	7
5	8	6
8	11	0
5.5	9	5
6.5	10.5	3
7	N/A	2
7.5	N/A	1
8	11	0
9	13	00
10	15	000
12	17	N/A
15	17	N/A
20	35	N/A
25	50	N/A

Quick & Easy KNITTING

Knitting kit bag

Needle organiser

When you've built up a collection of needles of all different sizes and types, storing them can become tricky. A needle organiser keeps them all in one place and protected against damage. Depending on your preference, you can get either a needle roll or a bag, which is like a long pencil case.

Pins

Useful for pinning pieces of knitting together when sewing up or pinning out to get measurements, pins with large heads are ideal, as they won't get lost in your work.

Point protectors

These will prevent the points of your needles from being damaged, as well as other things being damaged by them. Sharp needles will easily puncture bags, and fragile tips can be rather prone to breaking while being transported. Point protectors will also prevent unfinished work from slipping off the ends of your needles while you are not working on your project.

Row counter

Used to keep track of how many rows you've knitted, this is another helpful tool that will save you from counting the stitches in your work. There are different types of counters available; some sit on the end of your needle and can be turned at the end of each row, while others are available as a clicker.

Stitch markers

These can be used at the beginning and end of a panel of stitches, such as a cable detail, and to mark the end of each row when working in the round. They can be incredibly useful when you're following a complex pattern, and save you a lot of time by avoiding counting stitches on every row. When you get to a marker in your work, simply transfer it from the right-hand to the left-hand needle and continue.

Reference

Knitting bag
Available at most craft stores, knitting bags come with many compartments for storing all your tools and materials. They are usually made of sturdy material that won't be damaged by the sharp points of your needles.

Knitting needle gauge
It's essential to know what size of needle you're knitting with. If you're unsure, either because the needle has no marking or it has been rubbed off, a needle gauge will be able to tell you. All you need to do is poke the needle through the holes to find the best fit. Most will also feature a ruler to measure tension squares.

Scissors
You will need a pair of scissors for cutting off yarn and trimming edges. It's best to use a good-quality pair with sharp, short blades that will allow you to snip close to the work for a clean finish.

Stitch holders
Available in many different sizes, these are used to hold stitches that you will return to later. You can even make your own from a length of thin yarn or a safety pin.

Tape measure
A handy tool when you're knitting to exact measurements, you should always keep a tape measure nearby. Not only can you use it to measure the person you are knitting for, but also to check your tension and the size and progress of your piece of knitting.

Yarn labels

Everything you need to know about the yarn you're using can be found on the label, from weight and thickness to washing instructions

When you buy yarn, it will almost always come with a label around it. This label, which is sometimes also called a ball band, tells you everything you need to know about the yarn, from what size needles to use with it to washing and care instructions. If you think your project will need to use more than one ball of yarn, don't throw this label away, as it will help you ensure you get the exact matching yarn to continue working with.

Yarn weight and thickness

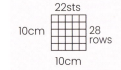
Tension (gauge) over a 10cm (4in) test square

Dye lot number

Hand-wash cold

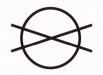
Do not dry clean

4.5mm (UK 7/US7)
Recommended needle size

Shade/colour number

Weight and length of yarn in ball

Hand-wash warm

Do not tumble dry

Symbols

Most yarn manufacturers will use symbols to indicate the properties of yarn and give further details about it. These will often include care instructions and tension (gauge). It will also include the dye lot. When using more than one ball of yarn in the same colour in a single project, ensure that all balls of yarn have the same dye lot. This way, there will be no variation in colour when you switch yarns.

Fibre content

Do not bleach

Do not iron

Machine-wash cold

Dry-cleanable in any solvent

Iron on a low heat

Machine-wash cold, gentle cycle

Dry-cleanable in certain solvents

Iron on a medium heat

Choosing yarn colours

You can find almost any colour you can think of, but how do you choose which one to use?

Patterns will suggest yarn weight and maybe even fibre, but colour is up to you. When choosing a colour for your project, you may need to consider more than just what it will look like. For example, as a beginner, you may find darker colours difficult to work with as you won't be able to see your work as easily. When you're using more than one colour, it's also important to choose colours that complement each other. A good place to start is to look at the colour wheel.

Using a colour wheel

This is used to see how colours work together. Each segment shows the hue (the pure, bright colour), shade (the colour mixed with black), tone (the colour mixed with grey) and tint (the colour mixed with white) of a colour. Blue, red and yellow are primary colours; green, orange and purple are secondary colours; and all the others are tertiary colours. Colours that are side-by-side harmonise with each other and those that are opposite on the wheel complement each other, and provide bold contrast.

Black and white

These are not included on the colour wheel as they are not classified as colours (black being an absence of all colour and white a combination of all the colours in the spectrum). When using black yarn to knit with, remember that your work will be more difficult to see and any complex details like cabling will not show up as well in the finished piece. When using white yarn, although every stitch will be clear to see, remember that this is not the most practical colour for wearable garments as any stains or dirt will easily show up.

Warm shades

Consisting of mainly red and yellow tones, the colours at the warm end of the colour spectrum can be used to bring richness and depth to a garment. Browns, oranges and purple are also a part of this group. A blend of warm shades can create a flattering garment.

Cool shades

At the cool end of the spectrum are blue, green and violet. Generally darker in tone than warm colours, their impact is lessened when mixed with these. If you need to balance a warm mixture in a project, you will need more cool colours than warm ones to do so.

Pastels

These very pale colours are extremely popular for babies' and small children's garments, and as such you will find a high proportion of soft yarns for babies are available in these colours. Pastels also feature strongly in spring/summer knitting patterns for adults.

Brights

Vivid and fluorescent shades can really liven up a piece, especially one that so far consists of muted shades. These colours make eye-catching accessories and intarsia motifs, and also look great when used to add a bright edging or set of buttons.

Knitting abbreviations

Confused about all those letters in your patterns?
Here's what they actually mean

alt
Alternate

beg
Begin(ning)

cm
Centimetre(s)

cont
Continu(e)(ing)

dec
Decreas(e)(ing)

foll
Follow(s)(ing)

g
Gram(s)

g st
Garter stitch

in
Inch(es)

inc
Increase(e)(ing)

K
Knit

K1 tbl
Knit 1 stitch through the back of the loop

k2tog (or dec 1)
Knit next 2 stitches together

kfb (o inc 1)
Knit into front and back of next stitch

LH
Left hand

M1 (or M1k)
make one stitch

mm
millimetre(s)

oz
ounce(s)

p
purl

p2tog (or dec 1)
purl next two stitches together

patt
pattern, or work in pattern

pfb (or inc 1)
purl into front and back of next stitch

psso
pass slipped stitch over

rem
remain(s)(ing)

rep
repeat(ing)

rev st st
reverse stocking stitch

RH
Right hand

RS
Right side (of work)

Sk k1 psso (skp)
Slip 1, knit 1, pass slipped stitch over

s1 k2tog psso (sk2p)
Slip 1, knit 2 stitches together, pass slipped stitch over

ssk
Slip slip knit

s
Slip stitch

s2 K1 p2sso
Slip 2, knit 1, pass slipped stitches over

st(s)
Stitch(es)

st st
Stocking stitch

tbl
Through back of loop(s)

tog
Together

WS
Wrong side (of work)

yd
Yard(s)

yo (yfwd)
Yarn over

wyib
With yarn in back

wyif
With yarn in front

[ ] *
Repeat instructions between brackets, or after or between asterisks, as many times as instructed

Understanding stitch symbol charts

If you're confused by stitch charts, there's no need to worry; they're actually simpler than you think

Stitch symbol charts provide a knitting pattern in much the same way as a written pattern – each symbol represents a stitch, and you follow it to make the pattern. Some knitters prefer them to written patterns, as they offer a visual representation of what a pattern should look like when it's knitted up and can be easier to memorise. When you come across a charted pattern, the amount of stitches to cast (bind) on will normally be provided, however, if it is not, you can easily work it out from the number of stitches in the pattern 'repeat'. Cast (bind) on a multiple of this number and any extras for edge stitches outside the repeat and you're ready to go.

In a stitch symbol chart, each square represents a stitch and each horizontal line of squares represents a row. After casting (binding) on, work from the bottom of the chart upwards, reading odd-numbered rows, which are usually RS rows, from right to left and even-numbered rows from left to right. After knitting any edge stitches, work the stitches inside the repeat as many times as required. When you have worked all the rows on the chart, start again at the bottom of the chart.

Stitch symbols

These are some of the most commonly used stitch symbols. However, different pattern providers may use different symbols, so always follow the explanations given in a pattern.

☐ = k on RS rows, p on WS rows

■ = p on RS rows, k on WS rows

○ = yo

╲ = ssk

╱ = k2tog

⋀ = sk2p

⋀ = s2k k1 p2sso

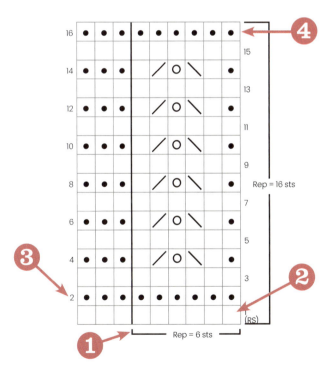

01 Cast (bind) on
The number of stitches you cast on must be a multiple of this repeat plus any edge stitches.

02 Right to left
Read row 1 and all other odd-numbered rows from right to left.

03 Left to right
Read row 2 and all other even-numbered rows from left to right.

04 Repeat
When you have finished the last row of the stitch symbol chart, begin again at row 1. Repeat the pattern until you reach the desired length.

Quick & Easy KNITTING

Stitch Patterns

Follow this fantastic guide to the different stitches that are available to you, and use them in your amazing creations

After learning the basic techniques of knitting, you now have the ability to create a large variety of stitches. These can be used to start making your own original designs and adapting other patterns to suit your tastes. You may recognise some of the more common stitches, such as moss (seed) and single rib, but there are a wide variety that will enable you to create any number of attractive items. There are just a few examples showcased in this chapter, so take a look through to see which appeal to you most.

Knit and purl stitch patterns

There are many stitches that you can create using just these two techniques, and most are simple to work and easy to remember. Although the majority of these will create a pattern that looks the same on both sides, those with a right side (RS) will have the pictured stitch on the front and a different texture on the back. These simple stitches are ideal for making scarves and blankets.

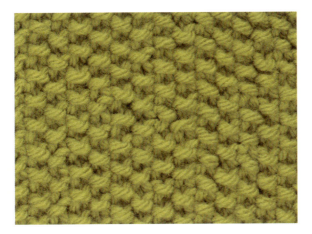

Moss (seed) stitch

For an even number of sts:
Row 1: *K1, P1, rep from *
Row 2: *P1, K1, rep from *
Rep rows 1-2 to form pattern

For an odd number of sts:
Row 1: *K1, P1, rep from * to last st, K1
Rep row 1 to form pattern

Half moss (seed) stitch

Cast (bind) on an odd number of sts
Row 1 (RS): *P1, K1, rep from * to last st, K1
Row 2: K
Rep rows 1-2 to form pattern

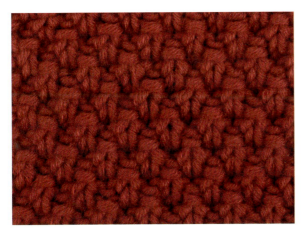

Double moss (seed) stitch

Cast (bind) on an odd number of sts
Row 1 (RS): *K1, P1, rep from *to last st, K1
Row 2: *P1, K1, rep from * to last st, K1
Row 3: As row 2
Row 4: As row 1
Rep rows 1-4 to form pattern

Broken moss (seed) stitch

Cast (bind) on an odd number of sts
Row 1 (RS): K
Row 2: *P1, K1, rep from * to last st, K1
Rep rows 1-2 to form pattern

> **Tip**
> If you lose your place while following a stitch pattern, start by looking at the tail of your work. If it is towards the bottom of your needle, you are about to knit an odd row (3, 5, 7 etc); if it is towards the top, you are about to knit an even row (4, 6, 8 etc).

Single rib

For an even number of sts:
Row 1: *K1, P1, rep from *
Rep row 1 to form pattern

For an odd number of sts:
Row 1: *K1, P1, rep from * to last st, K1
Row 2: *P1, K1, rep from * to last st, P1
Rep rows 1–2 to form pattern

Double rib

Cast (bind) on a multiple of 4 sts
Row 1: *K2, P2, rep from *
Rep row 1 to form pattern

English rib

Cast (bind) on an odd number of sts
Row 1: sl, *P1, K1, rep from *
Row 2: sl *K1b, P1, rep from *
Rep rows 1–2 to form pattern

Fisherman's rib

Cast (bind) on an odd number of sts and knit 1 row
Row 1 (RS): sl, *K1b, P1, rep from *
Row 2: sl, *P1, K1b, rep from * to last 2 sts, P1, K1
Rep rows 1–2 to form pattern

Garter rib

Cast (bind) on a multiple of 8 sts + 4
Row 1 (RS): K4, *P4, K4, rep from *
Row 2: Purl.
Rep rows 1–2 to form pattern

Basketweave stitch

Cast (bind) on a multiple of 8 sts
Rows 1–5: *K4, P4, rep from *
Rows 6–10: *P4, K4, rep from *
Rep rows 1–10 to form pattern

Little check stitch

Cast (bind) on a multiple of 10 sts + 5
Row 1: K5, *P5, K5, rep from *
Row 2: Purl.
Rep 1–2 twice more, then row 1 again
Row 8: K5, *P5, K5, rep from *
Row 9: Knit.
Rep rows 8–9 twice more, then row 8 again.
Rep rows 1–14 to form pattern

Little ladder stitch

Cast (bind) on a multiple of 6 sts + 2
Row 1 (RS): K
Row 2: K2, *P4, K2, rep from *
Row 3: Knit.
Row 4: P3, *K2, P4, rep from * to last 3 sts, P3
Rep rows 1–4 to form pattern

Increasing and decreasing

Using slightly more advanced techniques such as yarn over (yo) and knit/purl two together (k2tog/p2tog), you can create stitches with even greater detail and texture. These form more intricate designs that look great on their own or when combined with other stitches in larger pieces.

Basic chevron

Cast (bind) on a multiple of 12 sts
Row 1 (RS): *k2tog, K3, [inc in next st] twice, K3, sl K1 psso, rep from *
Row 2: Purl.
Rep rows 1-2 to form pattern

Herringbone stitch

Cast (bind) on a multiple of 3 sts + 1
Row 1 (RS): K1, *yo, s1wyib K2 psso 2 sts, rep from *
Row 2: P1, *yo, s1wyif P2 psso 2 sts, rep from *
Rep rows 1-2 to form pattern

Diagonal rib

Cast (bind) on a multiple of 2 sts
Row 1: *K1, P1, rep from *
Row 2: sl P1 psso, *K1, P1, rep from *
Row 3: *P1, K1, rep from * to last 2 sts, P2
Row 4: sl K1 psso, *P1, K1 rep from * to last 2 sts, P1, [K1 P1] into next stitch
Rep rows 1-4 to form pattern

Blackberry stitch

Cast (bind) on a multiple of 4 sts + 2
Row 1 (RS): Purl.
Row 2: K1, *[K1 P1 K1] into next st, p3tog, rep from * to last st, K1
Row 3: Purl.
Row 4: K1, *p3tog, [K1 P1 K1] into next st, rep from * to last st, K1
Rep rows 1-4 to form pattern

Reference

Glossary

All of the key terminology you need to learn to follow patterns and get to grips with the skills and techniques you need for knitting

As established, as set
An instruction in knitting patterns that means to continue working as previously established after an interruption in the texture or shaping. For example, an established pattern might be interrupted to work a buttonhole and then continue 'as set'.

Bar increase
See knit front and back (kfb).

Blanket stitch
A decorative sewing technique worked along the edge of fabric.

Block
A finishing technique in which the knitted piece is set with steam or water. Blocking smooths stitches and straightens edges.

Blocking wire
A long, straight wire used for anchoring the edge of knitting during blocking, most often for lace.

Cable
A texture in knitting that resembles knitted rope, made by crossing stitches.

Cable cast (bind) on
A firm cast (bind)-on edge made by putting the tip of the needle between the first two stitches on the left needle, working a stitch and placing it on the left needle. Although called cable, it is not related to making cables.

Cable needle (cn)
A short knitting needle with a point at each end used to temporarily hold a small number of stitches while you make cables. Cable needles are often curved or bent to prevent stitches from sliding off.

Cast (bind) on (CO)
To put the first row of stitches on the needles. This row is simply called the cast (bind)-on edge.

Cast (bind) off (BO)
Secure the final row of stitches and remove them from your knitting needles.

Circular knitting
When you knit fabric in a tube by working the stitches in a spiral. Unlike flat knitting, which is worked back and forth.

Circular needle
A needle with a point at each end and a flexible cable in between. Circulars can be used in circular or flat knitting.

Decrease
To decrease the number of stitches in a row.

Dropped stitch
A stitch that has fallen off the needle and is not secured. A column of dropped stitches is called a ladder.

Double-pointed needles (DPNs)
A knitting needle with a point at each end, usually used in a set of four or five to work in the round.

Duplicate stitch
Made by running a strand of yarn along the same path as existing knitted stitches. It can be used on the wrong side to conceal yarn ends or on the right side as a decorative element.

Ease
The difference between the garment's measurements and wearer's measurements. A garment with larger measurements has positive ease and one with smaller measurements has negative ease.

Eyelet
A single hole in knitted fabric, usually made with a yarn over increase.

Fair Isle
Refers to both the motifs and the technique derived from the colour knitting from the Shetland Islands and Fair Isle, north of Scotland. Generally, in Fair Isle knitting, two colours are used in each row, with the colour not being used carried along the wrong side of the work. Sometimes it can be used to refer to stranded colourwork in general.

Felt
Made from finished knitting by agitating animal fibre to lock the strands together.

Finishing
At the end of a knitted project, when final details are added, such as weaving in ends, sewing pieces together and adding buttons. Can also include blocking.

Flat knitting
When you knit fabric as a flat piece by working the stitches back and forth (unlike circular knitting, which is worked in a spiral).

Garter stitch
A reversible, ridged pattern made of alternating knit and purl rows. In flat knitting, garter stitch is made by knitting every row; in circular knitting, it is made by alternating knit and purl rounds.

Gauge (tension)
The size of a stitch, so how many stitches and rows fit in to make a certain size of knitting, usually ten centimetres.

Half-hitch cast (bind) on
A simple single-strand cast (bind) on. Stitches are made by twisting the yarn into a loop and placing them on a needle.

I-cord
Short for idiot cord, an i-cord is a narrow tube made by knitting every row on a double-pointed needle (DPN) without turning the work.

Increase (inc)
To increase the number of stitches in a row.

Intarsia
A technique used for working blocks of colour. The yarn is not carried across the back as in stranded colourwork.

Join
Either adding a new ball of yarn, turning a flat row into a tubular round or sewing pieces of knitting together.

Knit (k, K)
Specifically, to make a new stitch by working with the yarn at the back and inserting the right needle from left to right under the front loop and through the centre of the next stitch of the left needle.

Knit two stitches together (k2tog)
Putting the needle through two stitches and knitting together to decrease by one stitch.

Knit three stitches together (k3tog)
Putting the needle through three stitches and knitting them together to decrease by two stitches.

Knit front and back (kfb)
Knit first into the front and then into the back of one stitch to increase by one stitch. Also called a bar increase.

Knitted cast (bind) on
A cast (bind)-on edge made by working a stitch into the first stitch on the left-hand needle and placing it back on the left needle.

Knitwise (kwise)
As if to knit – with the yarn in the back and the right needle going into the front of the stitch.

Lace
Knitted fabric with an arrangement of holes.

Long tail cast (bind) on
A strong cast (bind) on made by using two strands of yarn: the working yarn and the tail.

Marker, stitch marker
A small ring or other tool placed on the needle to mark a location or stitch.

Mattress stitch
A method of sewing knitting together that creates a barely visible seam.

Multiple (mult)
The number of stitches or rows that are repeated in a stitch pattern.

Needle gauge
A tool used to determine the size of unmarked needles.

Pick up and knit
Draw loops through the edge of the knitting and place them on a needle.

Place marker (pm)
An instruction to place a stitch marker on your needle.

Plain knitting
Knitting without adding texture or colour, often in garter or stocking (stockinette) stitch.

Purl (p, P)
To make a new stitch by working with the yarn at the front and inserting the right needle from right to left through the centre of the next stitch of the left needle .

Reference

Purlwise (pwise)
As if to purl – with the yarn in the front and the right needle going through the centre of the stitch from left to right.

Raglan
A style of sleeve where the upper arm and shoulder are diagonally shaped from the underarm to neck.

Repeat (rep)
Repeat all steps between indicated points, usually marked by "rep from * to end".

Reverse stocking (stockinette) stitch (rev st st)
Stocking (stockinette) stitch fabric with the purl side used as the right side.

Reversible
A fabric with no right side.

Right side (RS)
The side of the work that will be displayed when finished.

Round (rnd)
In circular knitting, one horizontal line of stitches.

Row
In flat knitting, one horizontal line of stitches.

Selvedge, selvage
A decorative or functional edge. For example, a selvedge can be made by knitting the first and last stitch of every row, making them neater and more visible.

Set-in sleeve
A style of sleeve where the upper arm and shoulder are curved to fit around the shoulder and sewn into the armhole.

Slip slip knit together (ssk)
The mirror of k2tog: slip two stitches, one at a time, knitwise, and knit them together to decrease by one stitch.

Slip (sl)
Transfer the next stitch to be worked on the left-hand needle to the right-hand needle. Always done purlwise unless stated.

Stitch
A loop, either on a needle or in the fabric – the basic unit of knitting.

Stitch holder
A tool used to hold stitches that will be worked at a later date. Often shaped like a large safety pin.

Stocking (stockinette) stitch (st st)
A smooth pattern made of knit stitches. In flat knitting, stocking (stockinette) stitch is made by alternating knit and purl rows; in circular knitting, it is made by knitting every round.

Straight needle
A knitting needle with a point at one end and a stopper at the other.

Stranded
A type of colourwork where all the strands are carried on the wrong side of the work.

Swatch
A square or rectangle of knitting used to measure tension (gauge) or test stitch patterns.

Tail
The short end of yarn that isn't used.

Tapestry needle
See yarn needle.

Through back loop (tbl)
When making a stitch, put the needle through the back of the loop instead.

Twisted stitch
A type of stitch that's worked through the back loop.

Weave in
To hide and secure loose ends and the tail on the finished product.

Weight
When referring to yarn, weight is the thickness of the yarn rather than the weight of the ball.

Working yarn
The yarn that's coming from the ball of yarn and being used to make new stitches.

Wrong side (WS)
The side of the work that will be hidden when finished.

Yarn needle
A thick, blunt needle with a large eye that's used for darning yarn. It's also called a tapestry needle.

Yarn over (yo)
A strand of yarn placed over the left-hand needle to create a new stitch.